Journey to Heaven

Rachel Anderson

WESTBOW
PRESS®
A DIVISION OF THOMAS NELSON
& ZONDERVAN

WestBow Press books may be ordered through booksellers or by contacting:

WestBow Press
A Division of Thomas Nelson & Zondervan
1663 Liberty Drive
Bloomington, IN 47403
www.westbowpress.com
1 (866) 928-1240

Interior Image Credit: Danny Hahlbohm

Unless otherwise indicated, all Scripture quotations are taken
from The Living Bible copyright © 1971. Used by permission
of Tyndale House Publishers, a Division of Tyndale House
Ministries, Carol Stream, Illinois 60188. All rights reserved.

Scripture marked (KJV) is taken from the King James Version of the Bible.

ISBN: 978-1-9736-9682-7 (sc)
ISBN: 978-1-9736-9684-1 (hc)
ISBN: 978-1-9736-9683-4 (e)

Library of Congress Control Number: 2020912872

Print information available on the last page.

WestBow Press rev. date: 08/27/2020

CONTENTS

INTRODUCTION

Psalms 25:4 – "Show me the path where I should go, O Lord; point out the right road where I should walk."

I left God's paths for two 10-year periods in my life. Raised in a Christian home, my family was at church every time the doors were open. I was saved when I was 9 years old. At the age of 18, I left Bob Jones University in Greenville, South Carolina, after one semester, and did not darken the door of a church again until I was 28 years old. I thought I had enough church to last me a lifetime.

At 28 years old and the mother of a 2-year-old daughter, Kelli (whom I call Buddy), I knew that my baby girl needed to go to church and learn about God and Jesus and be saved when she was old enough to truly understand the plan of salvation. Isaiah 30:21 says: "And if you leave God's paths and go astray, you will hear a Voice behind you say, "No, this is the way; walk here."' I was finally ready to hear and heed God's voice. For the next 25 years, during which time our son, Nick, arrived to complete our little family, the kids and I went to church. Both of them were saved. Praise the Lord! I could never get my precious husband, Larry, to go to church with us.

When Larry and I became empty-nesters, I left God's path for another 10 years. When the grandkids were 4 and 5 years old, I knew that their dad, Nick, and I needed to attend church with them so that they, too, would learn about the Lord and be saved. Today they are saved. Thank the Lord! Psalms 25:10 – "And when we obey Him, every path He guides us on is fragrant with His loving kindness and His truth."

For quite some time I have felt compelled to write this book. Procrastination got the better of me as I had never attempted to do this and had no clue of where to begin and what to do. The Holy Spirit kept urging me to write, and I knew that He would help me finish this daunting task ahead of me. Over the years, I have saved writings of mine and some of Buddy's and Nick's, not knowing why I did so. Now I do, as they are interspersed throughout <u>Journey to Heaven.</u>

Psalms 5:8 came to mind one day: "Lord, lead me as you promised me you would…Tell me clearly what to do, which way to turn." At the same time, we shouldn't ask God to guide our footsteps if we aren't willing to move our feet.

This book may make you laugh, and parts may even make you cry, but most of all, I want the Holy Spirit to speak to you. The Lord your God is with you wherever you go; He will never leave you nor forsake you. We leave Him; He does not leave us. We all have our own unique journeys through life, custom-made for each and every one of us by our Heavenly Father. Seek His face, hear His voice, trust and obey, for His path leads to Heaven. Where will your journey end?

DEDICATION

I dedicate this book to

My celestial team, first and foremost: my Heavenly Father, precious Savior, and wonderful Holy Spirit. Without their help and guidance, I never would have written this book.

My amazing "True Husband," Larry, who resides in Heaven. God had our paths cross in New England, an Okie and a Yankee, all those many years ago. Larry brought so much joy to his family and friends and lots of material for my book.

My children, Buddy (Kelli) and Nick, who bring me great joy and pride. I won the lottery twice when they joined our family.

My grandkids, Cam and Princess (Sydney), who are so precious to me.

All of my siblings, especially my sisters, Joyce* and Nette, who inspired many stories in this book.

My BFF, Marsh, who listened patiently to all my "book talks" and supported me in this endeavor from beginning to end.

All of my friends and dear Sunday school sisters who gave me much needed feedback, as in Eloise's endearing words: "Come in from the pasture, and get crackin'!" I think that translates into, "Pick up the pace, and get 'er done!"

My author neighbor, Sharon, for her encouraging words that helped me to keep on going, even when I wanted to quit.

All of the hardworking, dedicated teachers around the globe who go above and beyond for their students every day. You are my heroes!

*In loving memory: 07/25/1940 – 05/15/2020

CHAPTER 1

The Journey Begins

I was born in Panama in 1948 where my dad was stationed in the Air Force. We moved to Dracut, Massachusetts, when he was transferred to Hanscom Field Air Force Base, MA, while I was still little.

I grew up there with 5 siblings, 20 years between the oldest and the youngest. I was right smack in the middle of us 6 kids with a big brother, George (Guy), 10 years older than me, and a baby brother, Benji, 10 years younger. My other siblings were a sister, Joyce, 8 years older, another sister, Jeannette (Nette), 16 months older, and Freddy (Fro), 2 ½ years younger. Who would have ever dreamed that the baby, Benji, would pass away first? In July of 2011, we lost him due to complications from diabetes. That was hard; we still miss him.

I am closer to Joyce and Nette probably because we have communicated with each other more over the years. Joyce taught me how to ice skate and roller skate, how to jump rope (AND Double Dutch), ride a bike, and play jacks. Nette watched over me, protected me, and was my perpetual playmate.

My parents were both survivors of the Great Depression, and they taught us not to waste anything. Every summer, Dad tended to his large vegetable garden. Ma canned lots of Dad's veggies for us to enjoy all winter. Dad worked hard at Hanscom Air Force Base, and

1

Ma kept a spotless home and cooked wonderful meals, homemade bread, and desserts for us every day. They also saw to it that we were in church every Sunday and then some. Ma was saved when a hairdresser witnessed to her before we were born and led her to receive Jesus as her Savior. That awesome experience was responsible for the salvation of our family. Wow! God is so good.

My earliest memory happened when I was nearly 3 years old. My mother was in the hospital after giving birth to Fro. Dad was home with us 4 older kids. Nette and I were in the basement with Dad "helping" him do the laundry. Back in those days, the early 50's, people had wringer washing machines, and I don't think that dryers had been invented yet, so everyone hung clothes up to dry on clotheslines outside. I was standing on a stool so that I could reach the clothes as Dad and I fed them through the wringer. I don't remember what happened next, but my hand went through the wringer along with the sheet I was trying to push through. It was a pretty awful accident, lots of blood, just so scary. I think that it affected Nette worse than me over time. I remember my sweet Dad bandaging my wound (trips to the hospital were rare back then) and rocking me.

When I was about 4 years old, we got our first TV, as that's when TVs became available. Our TV was in a small cabinet, and the screen was probably like 12" x 18"? Maybe even smaller! There was no such thing as color TVs back then; they were all black and white only. When Dad first turned it on tuned to the evening news, us kids ran to the back of the TV to see if we could see the "little man" inside! Everything was "live" back then, so some funny things would happen. One morning, Ma and I were watching *Captain Kangaroo*. He had a unique haircut, with thick bangs and hair one length below his ears. Well, I don't remember what he was doing, perhaps visiting with Mr. Green Jeans, but all of a sudden, Captain Kangaroo's WIG fell off!!! That was no unique haircut, it was a wig! Captain Kangaroo was bald headed! Ma laughed and laughed. They went to a commercial ASAP when that happened.

After a year or so, Ma decided that the TV had to go! She did not like the changes she saw in us kids. We would fight over what channel (I think we had 3?) we wanted to watch, played less outside, and we weren't reading as many books as we used to before we had a TV. So, she called the "junk man" and paid him a dollar to haul the TV away! I remember how unhappy my dad was when he came home from work and the TV was gone. It didn't take him long to adjust, sweet man that he was, and life went on as usual in the household. My siblings and I played outside for hours once again, and we'd walk a mile in the summers to our little country library and check out books to read. I remember Nette and me reading most of the classics by Mark Twain, Charles Dickens, the Bronte sisters, all the Nancy Drew books. When I would tell my elementary school students that we only had our TV a year when I was very small and that we didn't get another one until I was a senior in high school, the looks on those little faces were of total disbelief and probably horror, as well. ☺

Nette, Fro, and I all attended the same small elementary school in Dracut, Massachusetts. It only had 4 teachers: one first, second, third, and fourth.

Mrs. Garland, 1st grade, was and still is my very favorite teacher of all time. I can still see her sweet face. She made school fun. When I would go back to New England to visit family there, sometimes we would go to Phineas Street where Mrs. Garland always lived to see her. We exchanged Christmas cards for decades.

I think I was Miss Droney's pet in 3rd grade. Sometimes she would let me stay in at recess to put the cursive writing on the board for the children to copy. I wore my 2 big sisters' hand-me-down clothes, but Miss Droney made me feel special.

When I was in Miss Droney's 3rd grade class that year, I would sometimes hear kids across the hall cry out in pain when their teacher would rap their knuckles with a ruler. They may have been stinkers, I don't know, but I was terrified of the thought that she was going to be my 4th grade teacher the following year. So, I started praying each night when I said my prayers that I would not have to have this teacher the next year. The summer after 3rd grade, I had been running around playing with my friends. As I came up the driveway into our backyard, I saw Ma sitting in a chair reading the newspaper. All of a sudden she proclaimed, "Oh, my! You know that 4th grade teacher who was going to be your teacher this year? She died!" I didn't say a word, but I felt like I would surely faint because I thought I had killed her with those prayers of mine!!! I meant for the Lord to have her retire or move near family as she was quite advanced in years. I don't believe I ever told Ma the whole story, and for years I did feel guilty. After that, when I said my prayers, I learned to be *specific!*

My family and I lived across the street from an awesome pond. The pond was fun for us kids all year long. In the summer months, we'd skip rocks on it, or look for turtles, frogs, and polliwogs. To me, the pond was best in the winter because we got to ice skate for months on its frozen surface. New England winters can be quite harsh with lots of snow, so when we had blizzards, deep snow would cover our beloved pond, and ice skating, of course, was out of the options for winter time fun for a while. As luck would have it, though, when we couldn't skate on the pond, we could always go sledding down the hills! Yahooooo!

Sister and the Serving Tray

Dedicated to my big sister, Nette, and to all those cherished childhood memories, of which she was a part.

"Yeah! With a blizzard like this, we surely won't be going to school tomorrow!" I announced to no one in particular. My siblings and I had our faces pressed up against the icy living room window, staring out at the beautiful solid white picture that only God could paint.

My big sister, Jeannette, or Nette, as our family called her, stood beside me, nodding in agreement. Although close in age, only 16 months apart, we were very different. Nette was tall for fourteen with long, red hair and a temper to match. My height and hair were both shorter, and I had an even disposition. Sis was probably musing about the next wonderful book she'd be reading tomorrow. Me? No way! I had sledding on my mind at that moment. My two little brothers, Fro and Benji, had similar thoughts. All that snow (and it was sure to be 2 or 3 *feet* by morning!) meant building snowmen, forts, and choosing up sides for snowball fights.

Sure enough, the next morning when I jumped out of bed (something I would never do on a school morning, of course), the snow had measured up to my prediction of the night before: 32 inches of the sparkling powder!

"Ma! We don't have school today, do we?" I hollered down the stairs. Before waiting for her to reply, I ran back into the bedroom I shared with Nette and started shaking her awake. "Nette! Get up! There's no school today! YIPPEEEEE!" Trying her best to ignore me, she rolled over, slowly, and faced the wall.

The effort it took for my sister to roll over wasn't just because she was still half asleep; it was also because of everything she wore to bed in the winter! Nette was cold-natured, and our modest 2-story New England home had no heat upstairs where the bedrooms were. Our bedroom was SO cold in the winter that we could see our breath when we exhaled! When Nette went to bed, she wore her long-johns, flannel pajamas, two pairs of knee socks, a scarf, and a sweater! She also wriggled around in her bed so that she was totally engulfed in the covers, that is, all but her nose.

"Oh, well, guess I'll have to go call Pam and see if she wants to go sledding with me today," I muttered as I hurriedly got dressed. Once downstairs, I wolfed down a steaming bowl of Quaker Oats and dashed for the phone. "Pam? Hello, is this Pam?" I called excitedly into the receiver. Pam was my very best friend in the world and she was "mischievous as the day is long," as my dad would say. I looked up *mischievous* in the dictionary: "mischievous: inclined to annoy with playful tricks." Yep, that was Pam all right. Maybe that's why I enjoyed her company so much, because Dad also said that we were "two peas in a pod."

Pam told me that a big group of kids were sledding down Tommy's hill. Tommy lived up the hill and across the street from Pam. His family owned several acres, and on this land was a giant hill. I mean it was *steep*! I told Pam that I was on my way.

Pam's house was about a mile from mine, and we had both travelled that road many times before by foot and bikes, never minding the distance. This snowy morning, I pulled my flying saucer behind me. A flying saucer is an aluminum disk with handles on either side. One can *fly* down an icy hill in one of those things!

I picked up Pam at her house, and soon we were standing at the top of Tommy's hill. Lots of kids were already there. Pam had brought her old sled. We saw mostly sleds, saucers, and a toboggan, but there were also more creative means of transportation, such as scraps of linoleum, cardboard boxes, and trash can lids. We took a deep breath. Pam plunked down on her sled and dug her heels into the icy snow. I sat Indian-style in my saucer and pushed off with my mitten-clad hands.

Away we flew down that steep, icy hill! Faster and faster we sailed to the bottom, which seemed so very far away only seconds before. "Now *that's* what I call a **ride**!" exclaimed a breathless Pam. I noisily pulled up alongside of her in the crunchy snow and echoed, "Fantastic! Let's do that again!"

Pulling a sled or sled-like devices **up** that long hill wasn't nearly as much fun as it was riding down that terrifying descent, but it "all came with the territory," as Dad would have said. We must have made the round trip a hundred times that day, stopping for a quick bowl of hot chicken noodle soup at Pam's house for lunch.

We didn't have school for the rest of that week, and every day I picked up Pam on our way to Tommy's hill. We had **SO** much fun! If only I could talk Nette into coming. She hated the cold and would rather stay indoors and read, but I knew if she just tried sledding down that wonderful hill *one time*, she'd be hooked. So, I pestered her all week about coming with me to go sledding. I guess I finally wore her down because at the end of the week she said in a rather perturbed voice, "Oh, all right, I'll go sledding with you, but I'm only going to watch." I just knew when she saw how much fun it was racing down, down, down to the bottom of the hill, she'd have to try it for herself.

Remember earlier when I told you that Pam was mischievous? Well, we saw Nette standing at the top of the hill watching us race to the bottom several times. I knew it wouldn't be long before I could talk Sis into riding down the hill by herself. Pam had her own idea. Tommy had the misfortune of crashing into a tree with his sled earlier in the week, thereby rendering it useless for the time being. So, not to be left out of all that fun just because his ride was out of commission, he had run home to find a temporary replacement. I had seen lots of different means of traversing an icy hill before, but *never* on a silver serving tray!!! That's what Tommy had tucked under his arm when he came panting back up the big hill. His mom had let him "borrow" it. "Sure, sure," we all nodded in unison. Tommy had the last laugh, though, as that tray was without a doubt the *fastest* thing on the hill! Holy mackerel! He was nearly off the ground! Pam and I weren't afraid of much, but taking a turn on the silver tray scared us half to death! One time down that icy hill on Tommy's mom's "borrowed" tray was enough for us!

"Hey, Fluffy, I've got an idea," Pam said. "Maybe we can talk your sister into riding down the hill on the silver serving tray by telling her it's a once-in-a-lifetime experience". Hmmmm, not a bad idea, I thought. After all, Nette had dealt me my share of misery. It was payback time.

I walked over to Nette and said, "Hey, Sis, don't you want to try riding down the hill for yourself now?" I had asked her that same question several times that afternoon, but the reply was always the same: "I'm too scared; it's too steep," she'd answer. "Aw, c'mon, Nette, we'll find something fun for you to ride. You don't want to be a chicken now, do you?" That did it. "Oh, **okay,** but you'd better be sure it's slow." Right.

I ran over to Pam to tell her the good news, and she traded Tommy her sled for his silver serving tray. We decided to form a sort of train, putting the toboggan up front, several sleds and saucers after that, and we put Nette in the tray at the end telling her she'd be the caboose. We assured her she'd be so far behind the rest of us that we'd be taking a nap at the bottom of the hill waiting for her to arrive! HA! Pam hopped onto the toboggan with some other thrill-seekers, I jumped onto my saucer, the big boys gave us a push, and away we all went down Tommy's hill like a giant snake slithering across an icy mountain.

Seconds into the ride, I heard a blood curdling scream and glimpsed a white-faced Nette, mouth and eyes wide open, long red hair streaming behind her, as shew flew past everyone! She looked like Aladdin on his magic carpet! I swear that girl was airborne! I craned my neck to see around the others just in time to witness Nette's head narrowly miss hitting a huge boulder close to the bottom of the hill. Phew! Then she zoomed down a short embankment and was gone.

Pam and I fell out of our respective missiles at the bottom of the hill roaring with laughter. We laughed so hard I thought we were going to wet our pants! "Did you – see – her – go – flying by?" Pam shrieked between gasps of air. "**Did I**? Her hair was flapping in the breeze; it was **SO** hilarious!" I replied, still rolling with laughter on the freezing, icy ground. "Where *is* she? We'd better go find her," I said as I stood up and looked around.

There she was, about 30 feet away. At least I *thought* it was Nette. She had ended up further down the hill than *anyone* had ever gone before. She had her back to me, still sitting on that silver serving tray, her mitten clad hands tightly grasping onto the handles.

At the very bottom of this big hill was a brook. It never froze over in the winter because the water ran rather swiftly across the hill. No one had ever come close to landing in the icy water of that brook, that is, before **today**, before Nette rode down Tommy's hill on his silver serving tray. Nette was sitting in about 12 inches of frigid water. She slowly turned just her head around towards me, like one of those owls who can turn its head all the way around without moving its body at all. When I saw her eyes, I knew I was dead meat. I had seen that look come over her face before. Remember I told you that Nette had a temper to match that red hair of hers? That's when I had seen that look, when she would lose her temper and was about to go into orbit! All I remember of the next few seconds was grabbing my flying saucer, shouting, "**RUN FOR YOUR LIFE!**" to Pam, and scrambling up that steep, slippery hill as fast as I could propel my body! Something invisible must have risen up inside Nette, because all of a sudden she was in hot pursuit (or should I say cold?) and dead on my heels, wet clothes streaming icy water droplets behind her.

"I'm going to kill you when I get you!" she screamed after me. I didn't doubt for one second that she would! What usually took me about 20 minutes to walk home took me all of maybe ten, maybe less! Nette was chasing me all the way, yelling like a maniac the whole time. I never slowed down, not even when I saw the safety of home around the last corner.

I flew up the front steps and nearly ripped the door off its hinges as I burst into the house. "**SHE'S GOING TO KILL ME, MA! NETTE'S GOING TO KILL ME!**" I shouted as I ran past Ma cooking supper and into the bathroom, locking the door behind me. Before my mother could collect herself to ask what on earth was going on, a crazed Nette flew panting and ranting in the door herself! *"Where is she? I'm going to KILL her!"* Nette wheezed as she burst into the kitchen, wide-eyed, cold, wet, and furious. *Fluffy played a mean trick on me, and I'm going to make her PAY!"* she yelled as she started pounding on my hiding place. I was lifting a silent prayer to heaven on the other side of the door, a prayer that I would still be alive the next morning, and relatively speaking, in one piece!

Ma finally quieted Nette down, got her into some dry pajamas, and made her promise not to kill her sister, *me*! When I heard Nette reluctantly say, "I promise," I gingerly emerged from the bathroom and walked over to my big sister who was sitting at the kitchen table waiting for some piping hot supper. "I'm sorry, Nette. That was a mean thing to do to you, I know, but you have to admit, that serving tray can really *fly*, can't it?" I teasingly asked. Big mistake! Ma stepped between us and said rather disgustedly, "That's enough, you two. It's time for supper."

When Dad, Ma, Nette, my two little brothers and I were all seated around the kitchen table, Dad offered up the blessing. I peeked at Nette who was seated directly across the table from me. Bad idea. She was also peeking at *me* with that same crazed look I saw in her eyes while sitting in the icy water of the brook! I shut my eyes tightly and didn't peek again, let me tell you! All during supper Nette sat and stared at me as she chewed her food very deliberately. I did my best not to look in her direction. All I could think about was the fact that we shared a bedroom and that Nette was probably plotting to do something awful to me when we went upstairs!

Bedtime did inevitably arrive. Nette piled on all those bedclothes of hers, as usual, but *not* as usual, she gave me one long, cold stare before she turned towards the wall and switched off the lamp.

I laid awake in bed for the longest time. I sent up another prayer about being alive in the morning, just in case God hadn't heard the first one what with all that yelling going on earlier. I vowed I would **never** close my eyes and fall asleep again, the rest of my life, but of course, I did anyway.

Sometime in the middle of the night, I awoke with a start. I couldn't breathe! I was coughing and sputtering and sat bolt upright in bed. My nose hurt *so badly*! Then I heard an all too familiar laugh…Nette's. She was standing there beside my bed, in the dark, cackling with delight. "So there!" she said, "serves you right," and she hopped back into her bed, pulled up the covers and rolled over, still chuckling to herself all the while.

That pain in my nose? It was a *clothespin* that Nette had

clamped onto it! That's why I couldn't breathe! Boy, it still smarted long after I took it off, too. Oh, well, I thought as I drifted back to sleep, at least she didn't kill me like she said she was going to …

Would I ever play another trick on Nette again? You betcha!

The End

It seemed like every winter huge icicles would form and hang down from the roof. As it warmed up during the day, these huge ice formations would melt a little bit and droplets of water would fall onto surfaces below. The stairs from our front porch had several steps, a landing, and then several more steps to the street. At night, the water that dripped from these icicles during the day would refreeze and make walking on the front steps very treacherous.

My oldest sister, Joyce, who had graduated and was working, parked her '58 Chevy on the street. Once in a while, she would drive Nette and me to the high school getting us out of riding the bus. It was cool having a "hip" older sister with a hot car! Well, this was one of those cold, winter mornings when Joyce told us that she would take us to school. When Nette and I barely stepped onto those ice-covered front stairs, we nearly bit it! Thank goodness we had railings to grab onto keeping us from getting hurt. Joyce was always in a rush, and when she came flying out of the house onto the porch, Nette and I didn't have time to tell her to be careful. Big Sis hit those icy stairs and went down hard. Her purse flew out of her hand, and its contents spilled out everywhere. Her arms were flailing, and her rear end hit every step, I'm sure. Well, Nette and I were laughing so hard, not because she fell, but because of how funny she looked. You have to admit that it does look funny when someone falls. Big Sis was SO upset with us that she grabbed her purse and its contents, got into her ride, *and left us watching her drive away!!!*

Nette and I walked back inside the house and told Ma what had happened. I am sure that we were thinking we'd get to stay home that day. Right. Ma said, "Well, I guess you girls better start walking." Huh??? It was in the dead of winter and had to be 0 degrees if not colder, AND the high school was at least 3 miles away (Google Maps say 1.2 miles - No way! We nearly froze to death!)! My parents only had one vehicle, and Dad drove it to the base, so there was no arguing about our predicament. Nette and I walked to school and most likely were late, probably even got detention, which meant we also had to walk home since there weren't any late buses. We certainly learned our lesson: if you're going to laugh at a funny fall, don't let the person see you!

After graduating from high school, I attended Bob Jones University in Greenville, South Carolina, one semester. Not ready to settle down and study, my two big sisters paid for a one-way plane ticket to New Hampshire for me (how sweet was that?). We lived together with Joyce's 2-year-old son, my nephew, Ty. We had some fun times!

It was during this time that I met and married Larry, on Okie, who was stationed at Ft. Devens, Massachusetts, while serving his full-time commitment in the Navy Reserves. My sisters and I would laugh at his accent and make him repeat words. We weren't being mean; we just had never heard anyone talk like he did. I had to look on a map to see where Oklahoma was, and I could not believe that it didn't have an ocean!!! Larry and I married on Aug. 3rd, 1968, and then moved to Oklahoma that November. We drove, and when we crossed the state line, I thought for sure that arrows would start flying through the air and a herd of buffalo would stampede across the road! Seriously! I pictured towns looking like the one on "Gunsmoke" where people rode horses and hitched them up to a post before going into the saloon or general store. Was I ever surprised at how "modern" things were in the great state of Oklahoma! Phew!

It was payback time for me, as now people would laugh at my New England accent and make me repeat words. I thought everyone talked like New Englanders until I met Larry. Now I was in the minority, but it was okay, Okies are some of the nicest people on the planet.

Over the years, we would fly back to New England to see my parents, who lived on Cape Cod then, my two little brothers who also lived there, and Nette and her family who lived in NH. I am going to share with you the essay I wrote several years ago about the wonderful pond, Daigle's' Pond, in Dracut, Massachusetts. Go back in time with me...

The Pond

Nette is one of my big sisters, and she lives in New Hampshire. My other sister, Joyce, who lives in North Carolina, and I, a transplanted Yankee living in Texas, always have this incurable desire whenever we would journey "home" to New England to drive to Dracut, Massachusetts, and walk around our old, childhood neighborhood. Nette, who has lived her whole life in New England, was sweet to take us there. Soon we were winding our way down shady country lanes, travelling back in time, to a wonderful era in our lives.

Virtually all of my childhood was spent living in Dracut in a modest two-story home with my parents and five siblings. My town was not unlike many others in New England, with hills for sledding, lots of tall trees for climbing, pretty meadows for picnicking, and woods for exploring. But the one most memorable thing about our neighborhood was the pond, Daigle's Pond, to be exact.

The Daigle family lived catty-cornered and up the hill from our house. They owned all the property across the street from us, and in the middle of their property was this magnificent pond.

As my sisters and I parked the car on the side of the road, I sat there staring at our beloved pond, soaking in all the wonderful childhood memories of which the pond played such an integral part. Nette, Joyce, and I strolled over to the pond's bank, and as we three middle-aged sisters stood there, one by one we started reminiscing. "Remember the time those geese nearly froze in the ice on the pond that winter? If it hadn't been for Mr. Daigle getting in his rowboat and breaking the ice around them, they wouldn't have made it." Heads nodded. "I'll never forget the time I fell in!" "Me, too, remember when I fell in, too?" More nods, but by now, I was off on my own journey, back through time, to the peaceful 50's, Elvis, rock 'n roll, Eisenhower, TVs, hula hoops, and the pond. . .

It was summer vacation. The pond was teeming with life: muskrats, polliwogs, frogs, turtles, catfish, ducks, geese, dragonflies, and a stately white crane who took up residency there each summer for many years. They all were busy with their own activities. The marshy areas along the pond's banks sported cattails that would sway in the gentle summer breezes. Those welcome breezes would also cause ripples to move across the pond's once glassy surface. Ripples...who could skip a rock the best and make those perfect graduated circles?

Every night for weeks during the summer and up into the fall my family and I would be lulled to sleep by the bullfrogs' deep, throaty chorus: "Jiggerum...jiggerum...jiggerum..." Years later, when we moved to New York, we all had a difficult time falling asleep at first. Ma was the first to figure out why. "It's the frogs! That's what's wrong. We're missing the frogs singing us to sleep," and she was right.

One summer in particular in 1954, New England was hit with several hurricanes. Dracut was far enough inland to only catch the "tail ends," as Ma called them. Those "tail ends" could really pack a wallop, though, let me tell you! I remember in particular, Hurricane Hazel, a category 4. My dad was on another Temporary Duty and was stationed in Labrador for a year. Big brother, Guy, all of 16, was "the man of the family," as Ma called him. We all stood by the windows staring at the pond across the street. Hurricane-force winds blew over the pond driving sheets of water from its surface. Cattails took off! The tall reeds along the shore were flattened against the pond's undulating surface. All of 6 years old at the time, I voiced my concern to Ma that there wouldn't be any water left in the pond after

Hazel decided to move on. Ma reassured me that there would still be plenty of water left; the torrential rains would take care of that!

All of a sudden, Guy exclaimed, "You won't believe this, but the Rousseau's' chimney just took off!" They were our next-door neighbors. Bricks were flying through the air! Guy started laughing; he thought that was so funny. Then he said, "There goes the Daigles' chimney!" Guy heehawed some more. Ma was quiet because she knew what was probably coming, and it did. We all heard Bang! Bang! Bang! on our roof! Bricks were tumbling down, and *our chimney took off!* Guy stopped laughing when Ma told "the man of the family" that he would be on the roof tomorrow erecting a new chimney! And he was!

Along the pond's shore every summer grew the most delicious wild blueberries. Whenever Ma needed some berries for baking, she'd give whatever kids she could recruit a tin pail and tell them to please go pick her some blueberries. We really didn't mind, since we knew the reward would be another delicious homemade blueberry pie, blueberry cupcakes, or pancakes. I'm sure we never returned quite fast enough for Ma because we ate more than we picked!

A wondrous transformation of the pond happened every fall. The water would begin to freeze! It would barely be perceptible at first. As Nette and I would walk past the pond on our way to the bus stop each morning, we'd survey the water. Day by day, more ice would form from the shore to the pond's center. Every afternoon we'd stop on our way home from the bus stop and peer again at the pond's surface. Always, without fail, some neighborhood teenage boys would start daring one another to go out onto the pond's semi-frozen surface to "test" it for the others. Finally, one daredevil would take the bet and gingerly, haltingly at first, start slowly sliding away from the bank. The ice would crack, and bubbling sounds would gurgle underneath the surface. Water would start to seep up through the many tiny cracks. One by one another boy (*never* us girls! We were smarter than that!) would venture forth until one of them fell through. Shouts of laughter would ensue, the soaked and thoroughly chilled hero would emerge onto the shore, and we'd all go home with wild stories to tell around the supper tables that evening.

Winter was my favorite time of year, and Daigle's Pond was the main reason. Ice skating was now possible for four glorious months, from late November to nearly the end of March.

I learned to ice skate when I was about 4 years old. For Christmas that year, I received my first pair of ice skates, a pair of "double runners." They strapped onto my snow boots. Ma bundled me up so much that I could hardly walk, let alone skate! She also tied a pillow to my backside, held in place with one of Dad's old belts. That pillow cushioned many a fall during my fledgling days of trying to master the sport of ice skating. Master it I did, though, and for years it would be my most favorite winter sport. As soon as I got home from school, I would change into my play clothes, grab my skates, and head for the pond. My brothers and sisters and I always dreaded seeing the front porch light flicker on and off, on and off, as we darted across the ice, for that was Ma's signal for us to come home: it was dark, Dad was home from work, and supper was on the table. Sometimes we were having so much fun that we pretended not to see the flickering porch light.

Ma would come outside, cuff her hands around her mouth and yell, "Jo-eeeeeece!" She was yelling for big teenaged sister, Joyce, to come home with us in tow. Oh, she was SO mortified when Ma would do that, but never the less, it would happen again.

Crack the Whip was my favorite game to play on the ice-covered pond, especially if there were lots of kids involved and I was last! We would form a human chain by holding hands. After skating as fast as we could go, the next to the last kid would let me go, and I'd sail over that ice with the speed of Superman, praying all the while that I wouldn't end up in the reeds where the ice was never quite safe enough. Talk about fun!

My big brother, Guy, didn't heed Ma's rule once, never to skate near the reeds. He had a wicked crush on Shirley who lived on the other side of the pond. Shirley was older than Guy, and she probably didn't even know he existed. She wore the most beautiful skater's outfits when she skated, bright wool skirts trimmed with white furry material and matching sweaters and gloves. Shirley never skated pell-mell like the rest of the neighborhood gang. She actually *waltzed* across that ice, making figure eights and skating on one long leg looking like the most graceful swan.

On this particular day when beautiful, blond Shirley was waltzing across the pond, Nette and I were sledding across the ice as we sometimes chose to do instead of skate. Guy had caught sight of Shirley skating from our living room window. He came bounding across the ice and asked me if he could use my sled. Guy was ten years older than me, and my sled was far too small for a gangly teenage boy, but I let him borrow it anyway. Just as Shirley came gliding by, Guy took off running with my sled held close to his side. All of a sudden, he slammed the sled onto the ice, hoping, I'm sure, to end up in Shirley's vicinity. The only vicinity he ended up in was in the pond itself! Guy slammed the sled down hard and far too close to the reeds. The ice gave way, and down he went into the frigid water. Nette and I started screaming for help. You can just imagine how embarrassed my big brother was then and at the supper table that evening when my sister and I told the whole family how Shirley rescued Guy from drowning in the pond. My parents tried their best to bite their cheeks and not howl at Guy's misfortune.

We sisters kept reminiscing . . . "Remember the time that foolish man tried to drive his car across the pond that winter?" Joyce asked no one in particular. Did I? It was in the dead of winter, around suppertime. Ma was in the kitchen preparing another delicious supper for her family, and Nette, Guy, Joyce, and little brother, Fro, and I were all peering out the front windows at the blizzard wreaking havoc outside. We were all worried about Dad trying to drive the 30 miles or so home from Hanscom Field Air Force Base in the blinding storm. The streets were especially hazardous as several inches of icy snow had already fallen. All of a sudden, a car came careening down the hill and veered to the right, down the embankment to the edge of the frozen pond. It was quite steep where the poor soul had landed. The driver put the transmission in reverse. The tires spun wildly and made a tremendous racket, but nothing else happened. He couldn't get any traction at all! Meanwhile, Guy had hollered for Ma to come quick! Now all of us had our noses pressed up against the frosty windows, trying to see the car through the blizzard's fury. Ma turned on the porch light, hoping the motorist would come over to use our phone.

As if thinking aloud, I will never forget Ma softly saying, "You don't suppose he'll try to drive that thing across the pond..." for no sooner had she uttered those words than off he went! He was driving slowly to the opposite bank of the pond where he had the best chance to escape his predicament, about 50 yards away. Without warning, the ice began to crack, and even through the howling winds of the blizzard, we could hear the deep reverberations echo underneath the thick ice. Well, he *almost* made it. About three-fourths of the way across the frozen pond, the ice buckled, and the front of the man's car took a nosedive towards the bottom of the pond! Ma gasped, we screamed, and the ill-fated motorist came bursting through the cracked ice to the surface. He scrambled to gain access to safe ice while his car sort of sputtered before it disappeared into the dark, frigid depths of the pond. By this time, the poor soul had made his way to the opposite shore to look for a home seeking help. Ma stood there in her apron holding a pot holder and shaking her head in disbelief for the longest time.

Poor Dad, as his story revealed at the supper table that evening how he bravely maneuvered his way home in the blinding blizzard seemed rather bland compared to Ma's account of the unbelievable event that had just occurred.

A huge crane, the mechanical kind, came the next day and fished the man's car out of the pond for him. I'm afraid it was a little worse for wear by then. He was probably in the doghouse with his wife, also!

The end of March would inevitably come, and the pond would

begin to thaw. Kids and adults alike would clean and polish skates one last time and put them away 'til late fall. As the weeks would pass, the muskrats, frogs, and turtles would all resurface. The magnificent white crane would return, and the delicious blueberries would once again ripen in the warm summer sun.

"Hey, girls, I remember the time Denny, my idol, kissed me on the pond one winter. We were warming our hands near the fire and…" Memories of the pond will never be forgotten. As we turned to slowly walk away from our cherished pond, arm in arm, big sister, Joyce, asked the question we had all been thinking. "Was the pond *always* this small? Why, I remember it to be twice, no, three times as big, don't you?" "Oh, yes," agreed Nette, "I know it was much bigger than this." Is it love, youth, or faded memories that make things appear larger than life?

The End

It's interesting to think about where family members end up living. My siblings and I have scattered across America. Guy ended up in Florida with his wife, Fran. They have lived there for many years. Joyce lived in several states and even right next door to me a few years ago. She moved to North Carolina to be near her family. Nette has lived in her home in New Hampshire that she and her husband, Ed, built before they were married over 50 years ago. My hubby, Larry, and I built our house here in Granbury, Texas, in 1988; we shared 44 wonderful years together. I still live in our home. Fro has lived in his same home with his wife, Diane, in Sagamore Beach, Massachusetts, for many years. Benji lived in Buzzard's Bay, Massachusetts, before moving to Greenville, South Carolina.

I think about where I live. There is this saying in Texas: "I may not have been born in Texas, but I got here as fast as I could." That is how I feel about this great state. Larry and I and toddler, Buddy, moved to Abilene, Texas, in 1976. This is my 44th year here in this great state. I live in a wonderful neighborhood in Granbury.

My sweet church is like a mile away, and my neighbors are simply awesome. The Lord has also given me precious friends who check in to see how I am doing and to get caught up. Nick and Buddy are so good to call their old mother often. My Heavenly Father always takes care of me; I am *so* blessed.

CHAPTER 2

Buddy

B uddy was born in Oklahoma City, Oklahoma. Larry and I were married 5 ½ years before she made her debut, and we were *so* elated with that baby girl's arrival. Even though "Rosebud," as her daddy called her that first year, was his side of the family's 5th granddaughter (no grandsons), she got lots of love and attention as there hadn't been a baby in the Anderson clan for 10 years.

Buddy's given name is Kelli Anne Anderson, but she ended up with many more. From "Rosebud" came Buddy, Kippy LaRue, Rooser, Blondie, and Mrs. McFarland. Phew! I read a saying somewhere that said: "A child with many names is much loved." That was definitely true of Buddy. From day one, she had her daddy wrapped around her little finger, and me, too. She was one of the cutest little girls with blond hair and big blue eyes and her daddy's cleft chin.

When Buddy was nearly 2, we moved to Abilene, Texas. I called Buddy to dinner one evening when her daddy had come home from work. When she didn't come, I stood in the kitchen's archway looking at her playing on the floor. She said, "Can't; busy." I had to duck back into the kitchen, biting my cheeks so as not to laugh out loud. I'm sure she was mimicking me! So funny. Another time, she and I were going to the mall. When we climbed into the old red truck I drove, she announced: "We're two girls together, Mommy, two girls together." How dear!

Every night her daddy or I would read Buddy a bedtime story. One evening I was going to read to her. Before I could read the book I had chosen, I always had to read, **Cinderella,** to her first. Well, I was particularly tired this evening, so I decided to paraphrase some pages to speed things up. Right away, Buddy said, "That's not what the book says, Mommy! It says _ _ _ _ _..." and she quoted verbatim what that page really said. I thought my 3-year-old could read! She had memorized every single word of that book, let me tell you, and she was not going to cut me any slack unless I read it correctly and all of it!

Once, Buddy was riding around with her dad in our old, red Ford truck. I was dusting in her room and picked up her Pooh bear. Buddy adored that stuffed animal so much so that she had worn off Pooh's lips, and one of his ears was missing. I thought, you know what, I am just going to surprise Baby Girl and go to Sears and buy her a brand new one! So I threw her old Pooh into the trash can in the alley. The trash would be picked up soon. When Buddy came home, I showed her the brand new Pooh bear I had bought her to replace her old worn-out one. I will never forget how devastated she was. What was I thinking? I ran out to the trash can, but the trash had already been collected; Bud's dear, old Pooh was gone...forever. Buddy never really took to her new Pooh bear very much after that day. I learned a valuable lesson.

When Bud was 3 ½ years old, her baby brother, Nicky, was born. One of my favorite pictures was taken when Nicky was a brand new 3-day old. Buddy ran into the bedroom and jumped into bed close to him. The look on big sister Buddy's face is priceless. I believe she was thinking: "Well, you aren't exactly what I thought my baby brother would look like, but you're mine, and I love you." ☺

Then again, about a week later, she slapped Nicky's face when he was sleeping in his bassinet in the living room while I was cooking dinner. It scared me! When I ran in there, big sister was standing by the bassinet looking very guilty. Nicky's face was red, poor baby doll! After I rocked him and got him back to sleep, I rocked Buddy because I knew that she was hurting inside. For 3 ½ years she had been put on a pedestal and had gotten all the attention. Now it was the new baby who did. I let her know how special she was, that she was Momma's first baby and that she would always have a special place in my heart. She was my helper, too! After that, everything was all right.

Buddy loved her little brother very much, but kids fight. Sibling rivalry takes over sometimes. One day, after she and Nick had left the nest, I was looking for something and came across a note that Buddy had written to me when she was about 7 years old. Nicky would have been 4. In her little girl penmanship, she wrote, "Dear Mommy, I have to go away for a while because Nicky called me a dummy and a poo-poo." I harked back to the day...many years ago... When Buddy gave me her note, she had packed her bag and out the front door she went! I was really scared that she just might try to really run away! If Nicky had simply left it at calling her a dummy, I think she would have let it go, but when he added "and a poo-poo," that did it. I hid behind the drape in the living room window and watched sad little Buddy walk down the driveway. She made it as far as the neighbors' house next door before turning around and coming back home. Yeah! I loved on her and loved on her *and* had a talk with the note's author about how hurtful words like he chose could be. The kids made up, and all was well once again. After finding that precious note all those years later, I looked for 2 pictures of the kids around the time Buddy had written it. Then I took the original note plus a copy and those pictures to the frame shop and had one framed for Buddy and Nick for Christmas that year. They still have them hanging up in their homes today.

Eating dinner one evening when Buddy was in first grade, she told her dad, Nicky, and me about her day. First of all, her beloved teacher, Mrs. Dowell, was home sick, so the class had a sub. *Then* the sub's baby got sick, so they had to have a sub for the sub. Bud announced: "It was **SO *exfusing!***" One does not make eye contact with one's spouse when a little one tells a tale such as this! We're talking serious stuff here! Way too cute!

Buddy was saved while we were living in Abilene and attending Pioneer Drive Baptist Church. Knowing my daughter had accepted Christ as her Savior was one of the best moments of my life. When we moved here to Granbury, while she was a teenager in high school, she wrote her dad a letter about his salvation. I found it in Larry's top dresser drawer after he passed away suddenly from a heart attack in 2012. Her dad kept Bud's letter for over 20 years. . .

I don't know what it is about Buddy, but she makes me laugh. We would get tickled at the supper table during her high school years. Why? Who knows! What made this even funnier is that her dad never cracked a smile when we were carrying on, which made us laugh all the more! Don't get me wrong, here; Larry had a wonderful sense of humor. One night as we were getting out of control laughing again, her dad said, "I'm used to dining in elegance!" Well!!! That just made us laugh all the harder as I don't think that Bud and I had ever experienced that!

Buddy is a very gifted artist and photographer. She took all the art and photography classes available to her in high school and never wavered when it came to what she wanted to major in come college. After graduating from high school, Bud went to the University of North Texas in Denton, TX. During first semester in her freshman English class, she wrote a sweet essay entitled, "Fether," about her beloved dad. . .

Fether

An all-American, happy-faced boy's picture is on my nightstand. He is wearing a plaid, button-down shirt with glimpses of a white, Hanes tee underneath. Although I can't see the rest of this youngster's body, I can imagine his Levi's rolled up slightly above his tattered, Converse tennis shoes. In addition, this child's moon-shaped eyes gleam cheerfully at the camera while his smile extends from ear-to-ear. This delightful boy is my dad.

Today, Dad still looks like the happy-faced boy that he was years ago. He is never upset! Out of the eighteen years of living with my family, I have never seen or heard my parents fight. On the other hand, Dad has seen me yell, scream, cry, and express my depressed feelings. Consequently, he stays out of my way when I need to be alone, or simply makes me laugh when I need to hear some of his ridiculous jokes. Pop's zany sense of humor is what keeps me going.

It seems just yesterday I had a lot of time to spend with my dad. For example, I can still remember hugging him around the neck to feel his scruffy, five o'clock shadow against my face. Also, I can clearly recall going camping, fishing, and singing silly songs on road trips with him. Where did all of these years go? Time came too soon to snatch me out of Dad's arms.

One day I realized how much I meant to Dad, and how horrible it must be to let go of someone. I went out the night before I left for college. Henceforth, my curfew was one o'clock, and I decided to stay out all night with a good friend; my parents were always asleep when I came home, even when I would tiptoe in late. So, I thought that they would understand when I came home the following morning because it was my last night at home. When I came home at ten 'til six, I found Mom, hysterical, sitting awkwardly on my quilted bed; she was literally "worried sick." However, as I comforted her, all she kept saying was, "I am just so glad that you are alive! Go tell Dad that you are safe; he has been worried to death."

When I saw Fether, I noticed that his face had aged; he had deep wrinkles on the sides of his eyes and bags beneath them. When I hugged him, I couldn't believe that I was leaving that day. Furthermore, I realized that I would never be able to crawl up on his lap, sleepily, without a thought. I would never hear him say, "Make a hundred, and don't talk to strangers," as he dropped me off at school. I would also no longer see his fabulous face at my dreaded cross-country meets. I felt like I had missed so much and done so little with him. Looking at his face, I knew that he felt the same.

There is a picture of a girl with long, blonde pigtails on Dad's dresser. She is wearing a flowery, blue dress. This girl holds a blissful, innocent smile upon her face, and her eyes gleam cheerfully at the camera. She does not realize that her beloved nicknames (Rooser, Buddy, and Kippy) will be heard only when she comes home on selected weekends from college. Nor does this girl, who I was, know that one day she will be leaving the best dad in the world.

The End

When Buddy and her brother were teenagers, I never fell asleep until I knew they were home, safe and sound. I would doze on and off, wake up, look at the clock, and breathe a sigh of relief when I knew that they were home once again.

The night that she is remembering was one of the worst of my life and her dad's as well. Back in those days, kids and parents didn't have cell phones. I had no way to communicate with her once I realized that she was past curfew. By 2 A.M., I was calling her friends' parents, something I really hesitated doing, but I was worried sick about our daughter. Then I started calling police departments and hospitals. It was absolutely horrible. Oh, the joy when I saw her face! Her dad was overjoyed as well.

I cross-stitched this saying when Buddy turned 16 and started driving:

"I hear your footsteps down the hall. You are home again and safe. All the burdens of the day are lightened – and all the night noises. . .are music to my ears."

Buddy wrote another wonderful essay in the spring of her freshman year of college entitled...

Locust Summers

As I sat on the lifeguard stand, sweat trickled down my cheek and landed in my hand-held cup of water. I slowly pulled the faded green cup to my lips and was about to replenish my insides when an immense splash unwelcomely soaked and chilled my tan, hot skin. As quickly as goose bumps arrived on my entire body, I yelled, "Hey! Y'all cut it out!" to some boys lining up behind the diving board eager to plunge like cannonballs back into the icy water. One of them was my brother, Nick. He smiled his handsome smile and motioned to his friends with one strong, developed arm and asked them if they wanted to play a different game. As I put my hair back into a bun, the boys raced to the other end of the pool, and a group of youngsters began to play, "Name the Animal" as they frolicked off the board. One pig-tailed girl flapped her arms like a chicken and happily belly-busted the water; her friends soon followed as a cow, dog, cat, horse, and bear. While I watched them jump into the pool one-by-one, my stare began to glaze, and my mind wandered back to a time when I had pigtails, and my brother was small and toothless. . .

"Hey! Nicky, guess what I am?" I yelled to him as I hopped like a frog and with one giant "RIBBIT" leaped off the board. We had been playing "Name the Animal" for about an hour, and I could tell that he was ready to play something else.

"A frog," he replied unenthusiastically.

"Do you want to dive for pennies?" I asked. Mom has some in her purse."

His five-year-old scowl looked familiar, and I immediately knew that the answer was no.

"I want to play on the floatie," he said with a wide smile that uncovered his two missing teeth. I had lost my first tooth in the *third* grade, and my five-year-old brother had already been collecting coins from the tooth fairy!

"Sure," I replied.

We proceeded to play, "King of the Floatie," a game in which whoever can stand on the air mattress the longest reigns over the mermaids and sea kings until a challenger beats their time or until Mom yells, "Hey, kids, it's time to go!" It was now about two o'clock, and Mom had spoken these familiar, despised words. So, we packed up our stuff: towels, goggles, pennies, sunscreen, and flip-flops. Next, we trudged to Betsy, our big, old, red truck, and threw our stuff into the cab with Mom and hopped into the back. Then, we positioned our bodies side by side and looked wide-eyed up at the sky. We knew the fifteen-minute drive home better than the Scooby-doo reruns that we watched daily. By each curve of the road, limb of a tree, and stoplight that we passed, we could feel how close we were to home.

The soothing, rhythmic motion of the truck soon stopped underneath our cool, shadowed carport. Nicky and I jumped out of Betsy and routinely changed our clothes and recuperated by watching cartoons and eating popsicles.

"Do you want to learn how to ride a bike?" I asked. My brother, being strong-willed, adventurous, and yearning to be a "big boy," jumped up without hesitation. As we went outside, I thought about how old I had been when I learned to ride a bicycle. I believe that I was six or seven and had training wheels for a few weeks. Realizing the challenge, I grabbed my bike by the handlebars. It was rusty, old, and yellow. The seat was worn out and showed its insides through a few cracks and scrapes. Poking out of the handlebars were blue and white streamers, and a playing card was attached to one of the back spokes in order to make that horrendously thrilling noise that all kids want their bikes to make when they are pedaling. As I walked out of the carport with Nicky and the bike, two thoughts jumped into my head: his feet can barely reach the pedals, and Mom is going to kill me if he gets hurt! However, his fearless face and my quickened adrenaline enabled our adventure to begin.

We strode to the edge of the lawn and both stood on the curb with the yellow bike in the street.

"Are you sure that you want to do this?" I asked. He looked at me crazily and hopped upon the bicycle seat. Then I grabbed the back handle of the seat and said, "You pedal, and I'll run." The bike wobbled and was hard to keep steady, but in no time at all we were flying down the road. Soon, we were going so fast that I couldn't hold on any longer! So, I gently let go without him knowing, and watched my baby brother. He was going so fast!

"Go, Nicky, go!" I yelled. He didn't seem frightened because I had let go; the problem came a few seconds later when he needed to turn.

"Turn right!" I screamed. "Nicky, turn right. Right!" My brother, not knowing his right from his left, veered left – straight into a six-inch curb. Just as my mother came outside, Nicky's body flew through the air and scraped our neighbors' sidewalk. I began to see if he was alright, but before I knew it, he was on his feet begging me to run with him again.

My mother was astonished! While she stood on the front lawn and we repeated our act over and over, my brother became a bigger "human scab" with each fall. Around his thirteenth try, he ran into our next-door neighbors' garage door and cried profusely while he climbed right back onto the bike. Within two hours, Nicky became the world's first four-year-old bicyclist.

After our conversation-filled family dinner about the bicycle incident, it was too dark for any additional riding lessons. So, we decided to collect locust shells. We both put on black clothing and searched our neighbors' trees for those interesting, brittle shells. While we were filling our bowls, I thought about how fascinating it is when a locust leaves its old shell behind in order to become a new creature. Nicky would always pick the young, wet, slimy creatures up, but I preferred not to touch their slick skin.

Like the locusts, my brother and I also changed. When we moved to a new town, the whole family left its "shells" behind, but Nicky became the new creature. He told us to call him "Nick" instead of Nicky and spent most of his time with his new friends or lifting weights by himself. He still possessed strong determination and a fearless mind, and he used it in playing football, excelling in academics, getting involved in school clubs, and standing up to peer pressure. Even though I don't see him very much I . . .

. . ."Kelli, are you O.K.? You can't just concentrate on the diving board; you have to keep an eye on the shallow end, also." When the head lifeguard jokingly acknowledged my locked stare, I quickly turned my head and wiped my face a second too late to catch a tear that trickled down my face and into my faded green, hand-held cup.

The End

In the spring of Bud's sophomore year, she came home one weekend. During this visit, she had her dad sit down with her at the kitchen table. Our daughter proceeded to tell her dad that she wanted to drop out of college "for a while" so that she could go live in Colorado and "find herself." Larry told Buddy that he was on a retirement plan and her finishing college in 4 years was part of that plan. He told her that if she quit now, she was on her own should she want to go back and finish getting her degree later on; end of discussion.

Christmas break that same year, Dad, Nick, Buddy, and I gathered in the living room after supper to enjoy the fire and begin opening presents. Before we handed out one present, Buddy said that she had something to say and that she needed to do this now. The bar stool was already in its same spot as each year Bud would sit down and read the Christmas story from Luke Chapter 2. So, Bud sat down and proceeded to tell her family what really was going on that previous spring when she told her dad she wanted to "find herself." She cut classes on numerous occasions, didn't study, and ended up failing one course. Her GPA left a lot to be desired. This was our very capable daughter! She said that she was afraid to tell us because she thought that her dad would make her come home to live and commute to a closer university and live at home. That university did not have the wonderful School of Art that UNT did. Buddy buckled down, took a full load of classes, and also worked to save up enough money to pay us back for the class she failed in the spring. She said that she needed to prove to us that she could indeed make good grades at UNT and get back on track. Then she showed us her grades: all A's and a 4.0 GPA! She was emotional, and so were we. There were lots of hugs and high fives. We were SO proud of our girl's hard work and determination.

While attending UNT, Buddy met a sweet fellow classmate named Jaime. In May of 1996, our son, Nick, graduated from high school on a Friday night, and Buddy and Jaime married the next day. Phew! It was a very busy week with two big milestones happening in our kids' lives. Nick was on his way to the United States Air Force Academy soon thereafter.

Buddy graduated with a double major in Art Education and Photography. She taught art in seventh grade and in elementary school. One day she said to me: "Mother, they work you too hard and don't pay you enough to teach elementary school (which is what I taught), so I am going to go to grad school to teach on the college level!" About this time, in the spring of '99, after 3 years of marriage, Jaime and Buddy parted ways. Off to grad school she went working on her Master of Fine Art in Photography.

Buddy worked many jobs while going to grad school. She was really poor! I have a soft spot for struggling, poor grad students like Bud was. She would come home for visits with flapping shoes!!! I just couldn't let her live like that, so off we'd go to the mall on a shopping spree to get her the things she needed. When we would get home hours later, she would put on a style show for her dad.

Buddy's tunnel vision paid off. She taught at a university in Ohio for four years before landing a job in Chicago where she still teaches photography. Bud's photographic prints are in many collections around the U.S. She travels across America, lecturing, putting on art exhibitions and even teaches abroad in Ireland. She has also published some photography books. I am in awe of her talents and accomplishments.

Buddy married her longtime girlfriend, Betsy, on a trip to Massachusetts since not all of the 50 states performed such unions back then. Betsy is a sweetheart, so talented like our girl. Both of them are very artistic college professors, with Betsy's medium being sculpting. She even designed Chia Pets for that company! These girls amaze me with their talents.

Betsy is an important part of our little family. Larry felt that way, too. We went through a rocky time when Buddy first told us that she was gay. Jesus tells us to love one another, and He loves Buddy and Betsy very much. I'm already looking forward to Christmas when we will all be together. I just wish that the girls would let me win at Boggle, Scrabble, or Peanuts *once* in a while. I mean, I *am* a senior citizen after all! ☺

One year, Bud attended a self-help seminar. I was commenting on her dad's loud snoring on one visit, to which she replied, sharing her newest knowledge with me: "Mother, **be *one with it; embrace it!*"** This is a good phrase to use once in a while for a big laugh. ☺

When I would tell or say something that I thought was particularly funny, and Buddy obviously didn't, it would make *me* laugh anyway, and she would comment: "Just crack yourself up, Mother!"

If something does or does not appeal to her, she may say, "I'm diggin'it," or "I'm not diggin' it." ☺ Oh, and "Take a chill pill, Mother."

My girl, who simply adored her dad, took over helping me when he suddenly passed away. I was in a state of shock and could barely function. Both kids were awesome. Bud helped me with the obituary, the funeral service program, driving to Fort Worth to have a favorite picture of her dad enlarged and framed for his service, ordering a spray of flowers for the funeral, etc., etc. She stayed with me for about 10 days, and during those nights she would crawl in bed with me, knowing that I would be crying, and so we both cried and comforted each other.

Bud has taught me many things during my lifetime. One of the most important is what unconditional love means. She and I have had our ups and downs, and we don't always agree on certain subjects, but Paul says in Colossians 3:14: "Most of all, let love guide your lives. . ." I love my sweet daughter so much, and I always will. We're still "two girls together."

The Brother and Sister that Fought
Written by Kelli Anderson
To my family: Daddy, Momma, and Nicky

Once upon a time, there were two kids who always fought. The brother and sister were named Kelli and Nicky. They hit, scratched, and kicked; all the things you could think of.

One day Nicky said, "Nanny, nanny, boo-boo, you can't catch me." Kelli said, "I don't want to play." Then Nicky said, "If you do not play, I will hit you," and he did. She hit him back and she told and Nicky got into trouble. They made up and played and played and played.

The End

CHAPTER 3

Nick

Nick was born in Abilene, Texas. He is the first native Texan in our family, and he loves this state. Nick is the only grandson on his dad's side. Larry's folks, affectionately called, MaMa and PaPa, had 5 granddaughters before we had Nick. When Larry called his mom to tell her, "It's a boy!" MaMa said, "Don't you kid with me, boy!" She and PaPa were elated to get that grandson...finally!

I know that teaching elementary school was what God wanted for me. It was something I loved to do, and I got to stay home with my little ones every summer. Leaving them as toddlers when it was time for me to go back to school was so hard. I can remember peeling Nicky off of my leg at the church daycare where he stayed during the day, crying, and I'd cry all the way to school. As soon as I got there, I would call the nursery; his teacher said he stopped crying before I even left the parking lot! That made me feel so much better.

Before I had kids of my own, I remember a dear friend of mine, Glenda, had a little girl who was very attached to her security blanket. She had loved on it so much that there was very little of it left when she was 5 years old. I thought, my kids will **never** have a security blanket! Wrong! I made a green and yellow patchwork baby quilt for the nursery when I was expecting Nicky. That baby was SO attached to his night-night, as we called it. When he wasn't even a year old, he would pull himself up in his crib and make this little noise which meant, "Come and get me!" When I would pick him up, the security blanket came with him. Eventually I had to wash it. He started to cry when I took it away from him to put it in the washer. I held him up and showed him where it was going and reassured him that it would be okay. Same with the dryer. Nicky would play with some toys on the floor by these machines until his night-night was dry. When I pulled it out and gave it to him, he would lie on the floor with it held close to him, loving and loving on it. Larry and I both thought that it just might go to college with him one day. Finally, when Nicky was in the 2nd grade, he gave it up. I had patched that thing so many times, it was ready to be retired.

When Nicky was 3 years old, he told his 6-year-old sister, Buddy, and me that he was going to marry us both when he grew up. Too dear! He would also say, "It's fonny." when he wanted me to **think** that something he did was funny. I might say, "Nicky, you did not straighten up your room like I asked you to do." He'd reply, "It's fonny!" Excuse me? I don't think so!

We had an alley behind our little home in Abilene. Our first wooden fence had slats placed in a horizontal pattern. Nicky could climb that fence in a lightning minute when he was little. The trash truck came down the alley to pick up trash. I swear that Nicky could hear that big truck coming a mile away. He would announce, "The trash can man is coming!" and off he would run for the backyard fence. Nicky's idol was the trash can man. One day when he was standing on the top slat and the trash truck stopped for our trash, I heard Nicky say to his idol, "I'm going to be a trash can man when I grow up!" ☺ How precious!

Breaking bones and having multiple sets of stitches, Nick helped me to turn gray early. He was a fearless kid, and he had to find out the hard way that wearing a Superman cape didn't make one fly when one jumped out of a tall tree! That was his first broken bone. . .

Nick was saved when he was 10 years old. Praise the Lord! Being saved as a child is so awesome.

In 8th grade, Nick's English teacher had the class write a caring essay. I saved it all these years, not knowing that I would be sharing it with you in Journey to Heaven.

Caring Essay: My Mother

As she keeps scrubbing the bathrooms and dusting the furniture, she thinks about her children. She imagines her son playing ball on the cool, fall field at the local recreation area. Her daughter is probably at one of the fad-loving shops at the urban mall. She is the salesman's wife who has recently lost his job. As she continues her thankless job, she wonders what the future will bring.

Father has come home from golf, and the kids begin to wash for dinner. She pulls the warm dinner out of the oven. She is monotonously thanked for her hard, unappreciative work. She eats little and waits for her family to finish their meal.

As she clears off the table and begins to unload the dishwasher, she wonders if she will have to sleep on the couch tonight. She can no longer tolerate the loud snoring of her husband. She feels badly leaving his side; however, she cheerfully carries on with her routine. She knows that he sometimes should be the one struggling for rest on the uneven lumps of the couch. Still, she never complains.

She sits down for the first time this evening and begins to work on her newest wall hanging. She has the skilled touch of the sewer's hand. She is once again lost in her thoughts, wondering how her fourth-grade class will behave on the approaching weekday. Sadly, she thinks of the shuttered home lives of some of her pupils. Suddenly she realizes there is still work to be done, and she begins another load of wash.

The knock on her daughter's bedroom door is heard, and she enters the tearful room. She comforts her daughter and makes her realize that the stressful problems of teenage high school society are not all what they seem. A small hint of a smile can be seen on her daughter's refreshed face.

She checks on the family dog, giving him food and water and gently caressing the dog's thin fur. She tries to coax him into believing that he is the greatest dog on the face of the earth. Observing the sad expression on the beagle's face, she knows it is his normal expression, but somehow it still puzzles her.

As the day comes to an end, she thinks of tomorrow. She must make sure to set her alarm for church in the morning. She has taught her kids to be good, God-fearing, Christian individuals. She knows that someday when her children have kids, her good deeds will finally be appreciated.

Her day is over. She feels good about the endless chores and comforting memories that seem to routinely occur. Her children's lives seem to be going by too fast. Soon her daughter will be in college and her son in high school. Her thoughts and worries begin to fade. She knows that the problems of tomorrow can never come close to breaking apart the love that is shared between her family. She, of course, is my mother.

The End

When Nick was 16 and driving, he got a speeding ticket on the way home from school. The speed limit on this 2-lane road was 40 mph, and most people, I'm sure, went 50 or higher. Still, the law is the law. I accompanied Nick to the see the judge. I wanted him to know what a fine, upstanding young man that my son really was, so I proceeded to tell him! Well, the judge looked at Nick and asked him what kind of grades he made (Nick was a sophomore at the time). Nick told him all A's, so the judge came up with a plan. He would recuse the ticket *if* Nick made all A's all year! I didn't dare look at my son's face…yikes! Judge Macon told Nick to bring his report card by his office every 6 weeks when report cards came out.

On the way home, Nick said to me, "Way to go, Mother! I could have taken defensive driving and be done with it, but oh, no. You had to go on and on to the judge about how good your boy is, blah, blah, blah…Now I have to make all A's all year taking AP courses, no pressure…no pressure…" I did feel badly, but the damage had already been done. So, Nick showed the judge his next two report cards with all A's, and Judge Macon was so nice to tell Nick that he did not have to come back again. Phew!

Nick worked hard in high school. His goals were to make the Top 10 students in his senior class of over 300 and to be nominated to the United States Air Force Academy. He succeeded in accomplishing both. After Nick graduated from high school, he went to the Air Force Academy. He works in defense now and enjoys his job. I am so proud of his work ethic, being a great dad instilling Christian values in his children, and coming back to the Lord's path for his life. Nick, his son, Camden, and his daughter, Sydney, were all baptized in Lake Granbury by his church's minister. I had the privilege to see this happen. It was very touching, to say the least. Thank you, Jesus!

Riding with me recently on the way to pick up his kids, my grandkids, I didn't realize that my lovely instrumental music had been playing on the radio for quite some time. When I asked him if he'd like to change the station, he said under his breath, "What I'd give for your ice pick about now." I'm not sure if he was thinking about hurting himself or my stereo! Kids. They need to adopt an appreciation of smooth, calming music in their lives sometimes. Man! I should have replied to his response with, "Nick, *just be one with it; embrace it!*" ☺

Like his sister, Nick was an unbelievable help to me after his dad passed away so unexpectedly. I was so numb and could barely function at all. Nick made a big list and helped me to sell his dad's vehicle and boat, getting several death certificates, helping me with finances, and on and on. I don't know what I would have done without his and Buddy's help. They were both so amazing.

Nick wrote another paper called, "Dad," two days after his beloved father passed away. I will include it in the last chapter.

God richly blessed me with my daughter, Buddy, son, Nick, and grandkids, Cam and Princess. They mean the world to me. Knowing that I will get to spend eternity with my family in heaven is such an amazing gift from God and Jesus. I am *so* blessed.

CHAPTER 4

The Grandkids

Camden

I can't believe that Cam, our first grandchild, is 15 years old. Where did the time go? I told him the other day that Gramma needed to put a brick on his head to keep him from growing up so fast! Cam was the cutest baby and is so handsome now.

From the time Cammie was a toddler, Grampa was his favorite. He and Princess thought Grampa hung the moon. When Cam was 14 months old, he was walking with Grampa, holding his hand. I ran to catch up with them so that I could hold Cammie's other hand. He pushed my hand away; he was *only* going to hold his Grampa's. Well! I knew where I stood alright.

When Cammie started talking, he had some mispronunciations. We figured out the "code:" Gr became Br (so Larry and I became "Bramma" and "Brampa"), cr was pr, and sl was fw. Phew!

Cammie was 3 or 4 when this story happened. On a trip to NC to see Nick and his family, Cammie and Princess, his baby sister, were upstairs in their rooms sleeping. We adults were also upstairs in the hall talking quietly (or so we thought) on our way to the playroom. All of a sudden, Cammie comes out of his room in his Spider Man shorty pajamas, hands on hips, and says: "What's the *big* idea? You're being too *loud*! I'm trying to FWEEP! I'm trying to FWEEP!" Then he turns and marches back into his room and closes the door. The 4 of us bolted for the playroom and had a big laugh, quietly, mind you.

Every time we visited the little Anderson family, I would bring both Cammie and Princess a new outfit. It was very thoughtful of their mother to put them on the children while we were there. Cammie walked into the den one morning sporting his new plaid shorts and polo shirt. When I asked, "Oh, Cammie, who bought you that new outfit?", he boldly announced to his Grampa, Auntie Kelli, and me, "*Brampa* did, and he *made* it!" Can the pedestal get any higher than that? I can't win...

When the grandkids were 4 & 5, their dad (our son, Nick) took them to the pool one afternoon. Cammie told me all about what happened when they got home. Nick went to reapply sunscreen, deciding to try the new spray bottle. Cammie said, "We got some in our eyes, Bramma, and we *pried! We pried, Bramma*!!!" Nick felt so badly.

Cammie and Princess used to like to play the Old Maid card game with us. Cam had a hard time not laughing when someone chose the Old Maid from his hand. So, his dad told him that he needed to have a poker face when that happened. The problem was that Daddy didn't explain what that meant. Cammie ended up with the Old Maid again, and when his sister pulled it from his hand, he went into *his* poker face mode making these grotesque facial gyrations! It was scary looking! We all had a big laugh. ☺

Last summer Nick took the kids to Six Flags over Texas, a huge amusement park. I told them to stay close to their dad, not to wander off nor trust any strangers, even an old woman like their Gramma, should she coax them to go somewhere with her. Cam said, "I'd ask her, 'What's in it for me?'" Cam's sense of humor is blossoming. He is very smart and an excellent soccer player (I may be just a little proud of him). ☺

Princess

My granddaughter's given name is Sydney, but I have always called her Princess. So far, she hasn't corrected me; we'll see how long that lasts. Princess has beautiful green, almond-shaped eyes and is pretty as a Princess, for sure. She is very smart like her big brother (16 months older), Cam, very artistic, a fine dancer, singer, and acrobat.

When Princess was little and she would preface what she was about to say with this phrase, "And not in a bad way, Gramma...," it was always a zinger about my skin. "And not in a bad way, Gramma, but the reason you get so many mosquito bites is because you have a lot of skin." Isn't that priceless?

When Princess would use this preface, "I don't know how it happened, Gramma...," #1, she knew, and #2, she did it. I would hold my breath. I have some decorative, porcelain pieces around the house that I have told the grandkids not to touch as they are very breakable and some are sentimental. There are plenty of toys here for them to enjoy. We had a precious beagle for 12 years named Doony, and I had a miniature porcelain beagle that I would move around into different displays. One day Princess said, "I don't know how it happened, Gramma (Oh, help me, Lord!), but Doony doesn't have a tail anymore." Well! I asked her if perhaps the reason why Doony didn't have a tail anymore *might* be because she was playing with him? Princess always owned up, so she nodded her head affirmatively. On another visit, she said, yet again, "I don't know how it happened, Gramma, but Doony only has 3 legs now." Have mercy! Then came the same question from me and Princess's confession.

Princess loves the flabby skin on my upper arms. She was swaying it recently, and I told her that she needed to be feeling my bicep muscle from working out in the gym. She replied, "But this is so soft, Gramma, and everyone loves it!" I don't *think* so, but how sweet was that?

Princess absolutely loves potatoes: mashed, baked, in potato soup, fries, etc. She is a connoisseur of them, and Bob Evans mashed potatoes in the refrigerated section of the grocery store is near the top of her list. Her mom's potatoes are #1.

Sometimes her dad does something special with the grandkids. When Nick takes Cam to a football game, Princess has what she calls a, "Party Girl Day" with me. We go see a movie, munching on popcorn and drinking Cokes. Then it's off to our local Cotton Patch restaurant because they have lots of potatoes! The waitress always looks at me when Princess orders a baked potato, some mashed potatoes, and a delicious bowl of potato soup. I tell her that my granddaughter will eat all of them! After her potato feast, we drive back to Gramma's to watch a movie while I give her a manicure and a pedicure. When I finished her pedicure the first "Party Girl Day," she popped up and announced, "And now it's time for my *massage*!!!" I asked, "Well, what about *my* massage?" She gave me one, all right, like about 3 seconds long. I think her nickname fits her well, don't you? ☺

CHAPTER 5

Church Memories

T he first church I can remember attending with my family was Collinsville Union Church in Dracut, Massachusetts. This would have been during the 1950's and early 1960's.

My church was little. There were only 14 pews, 7 on one side of the aisle, and 7 on the other side. The "regulars" sat in their same spots every service. We were the Fischer family, and we sat in the next to the last pew on the right. The Hammond family sat in the second pew on the right, etc. I'm not sure about this, but I think there were about 8 people in the choir?

Pastor Lehman was our preacher, and his wife was my Sunday school teacher. She was awesome. She taught us two acrostics that I have never forgotten. They are:

Jesus first	**God's**
Others second	**Riches**
Yourself last	**At**
JOY	**Christ's**
	Expense
	GRACE

Both of these are so true.

While attending church in Massachusetts, I remember 3 incidents that happened. One was when my sister, Nette, and I were like 6 and 7 years old. I wrote a children's story about one, and I will include it in this chapter. The other two I will share with you now.

My family attended church every time the doors were open, which included evening service on Sundays. One Sunday night, I sat on the left side of the aisle with David Lehman, the preacher's son, who was about my age. We were probably 10 or 12 or so. Anyhow, Pastor Lehman was preaching, and David and I were drifting away from the sermon, sad to say, because I am sure that it was good; it always was. Well, I found a pill either on the pew or the floor. Back in those days, some pills came in rubbery capsules with liquid inside of them. Curiosity got the best of us when I produced a pin to see what was inside of this pill. I'm sure that our heads were close together and that we had all but forgotten that we were in **church**! David was probably in big trouble when he got home that night as I believe his dad was well aware of his inattentiveness to the sermon. So, I stuck the pill with my pin, squeezed it (big mistake!), and out came this **stinky, stinky** liquid that shot into the air **and landed on Tori Elwell's neck in the pew in front of ours!!!** We both watched in disbelief as the disgusting liquid started sliding down Mrs. Elwell's neck, totally unbeknownst to her! She must not have felt it, but several people started looking around for the source of that horrific smell.

Another incident at this sweet little church happened when my sis, Nette, and I were teenagers. At evening service that Sunday, we had a guest speaker, a very rare occasion for us to enjoy. Well, Nette and I, and two other sisters, Janet and Judy, were going to sing as a quartet that evening. We were standing in front of the church with Judy and I in front because we were shorter, and Nette and Janet in back. Peggy, the church pianist, was playing the piano for us. I don't remember what happened, but Nette, Janet, and I got tickled. We could **not** get our composure back; hysterics had set in! Peggy played her interlude, and when it was time to sing the last verse, the 3 of us could not join in as we were laughing too hard, but Judy started singing her *alto* part, by herself!!! When I saw the expression on Ma's face, I knew that I was dead meat when we got home. It was awful. I'm sure the congregation was mortified because of our behavior in front of a *guest speaker*!

The third incident that happened at church took place before evening service began. I will include the short story I wrote about that important event here.

God's Nickel

Dedicated to my mother who taught her children to always do the right thing.

I grew up in a family of 6 kids in a small New England town. Money was tight, and there was little left over for extras.

On Sunday nights between youth and evening services, every so often Ma would give my big sister, Nette, and me two nickels: one for the offering during evening service, and the other to spend on penny candy at Polly's Variety, the wonderful candy store on the corner. This was a real treat for Sis and me. We had just enough time to run to the store, choose our 5 pieces of candy, and hurry back to church.

On this particular Sunday evening, Nette and I were happily running to Polly's store with our nickels when I suddenly tripped and fell down. I dropped one of my nickels, and it rolled into a rain gutter. Sis and I ran over to it. Getting down on our bellies, we peered into the gutter. There was the shiny buffalo nickel about 3 feet below, just out of arm's reach. There was absolutely nothing we could do to retrieve that coin. To this day, I can remember looking skyward and saying, "Well, God, I am *so* sorry *your* nickel rolled into the rain gutter."

Nette and I went on to the candy store, and we each chose 5 of our favorite treats, skipping back to church while we enjoyed our candy. When the offering plate was passed down our pew later on during the church service, I did not have God's nickel to place in it. *His* nickel had rolled into the gutter, remember? Or did it?

I felt very badly the rest of the evening. I knew I had not done the right thing. If I had, I would have gone without getting penny candy with *my* nickel, and God's nickel would have made its way into the offering plate. Nette probably would have shared *one* piece of her candy with me, and I wouldn't have ended up with a belly ache due to my conscience bothering me.

I was probably about 8 years old when this incident happened. I did not tell my mother what I had done until she was in her 80's. I told her that I had asked God to forgive me that night, and now I was asking her. Of course, she did, too.

I learned a valuable lesson that day, many years ago, a lesson that has stayed with me all these years: **DO THE RIGHT THING.** No matter what. You might be thinking that it was only a nickel, but it was God's nickel, one I can never replace. Life is all about choices. Make wise decisions.

Proverbs 3:6 - "In everything you do, put God first, and He will direct you and bless your efforts with success."

The End

In my New England neighborhood, most people spoke French and were Roman Catholic. My family may have been the only Protestants on our street. One weekend, I got to spend the night with my friend, Pam. She and her family had moved to Lowell, a town next to ours. Pam had to go to confession, so we walked to the neighborhood church. On the way, Pam said, "Help me think of some sins." I asked her if she and Ronnie, her big brother, had fought, and she replied affirmatively. When we walked inside her church, I saw this man leaning over what I thought was a bubbler

(Yankee talk for a drinking fountain) getting a drink. I was thirsty from our walk, so when he walked away, I went over to refresh myself with a cool drink of water. I thought this was a strange bubbler as the water was already there in a basin, not moving. Oh, well, I was so thirsty, so I bent down, cupped my hands, and had myself a nice, cool drink. When Pam noticed what I was doing, she nearly died! "What are you doing?" she asked me. "You just drank the holy water!!!" Yikes!

I had another wonderful Sunday school teacher when the kids and I attended Pioneer Drive Baptist Church in Abilene, Texas. Her husband, like mine, did not go to church. When she went back home after church, she was not a happy camper about his absence. One Sunday he said to her, "Well, I can see that *you've* gotten a lot out of church." That did it. From then on, she came home in a good mood. Her being sullen had a negative influence on her husband going to church. I knew that being cranky or nagging Larry would not work, either. This wonderful teacher, whose name I can't recall, also told me something else that was very important. When I used to pray before she shared this with us, I would start out by asking God to forgive me of my sins and thank Him for my blessings. She told us to *name* those sins. OUCH! From then on, I have. I also name some of my blessings; if I tried to name them all, I would never finish a prayer because my blessings are far too numerous.

We moved to Granbury, Texas, in 1988. Buddy was 14, and Nick was 10. We joined our new church that year, and I started going to Janie's Sunday school class then. It is a wonderful ladies' class. Janie is an awesome Sunday school teacher, and we have a special group of women who love and support each other. Janie has taught me many things over the years. I will share a couple with you. One of her sayings is: "Just because you can, doesn't mean you ought to." How true is that! This is a great saying for parents of teens to share with them – ha! My favorite saying of Janie's, a quote by Ravi Zacharias that she can recite it by heart, is this description of sin:

Sin

Sin shows you the beginning, never the end,
Shows you the pleasure, never the pain,
Sin takes you farther than you want to go,
Keeps you longer than you want to stay,
Costs you more than you want to pay.

It is SO true. Another dear Sunday school sister, Carola, shared this with us one Sunday: "An excuse is a lie disguised as a reason." Think about that; another wow! And just recently, Brenda shared this verse with us: "Bad company corrupts good morals." Sad, but true. . .

I will share two stories with you here about the grandkids. In this first one, the grandkids were 5 and 6. Nick and I were in "big church" with the kids one Sunday. When the congregation would stand up to sing, pray, whatever, Cam and Princess did not. I motioned for them to do so, and ***Princess gave me the stink eyes!!!*** Soon afterwards, it was time for kids to go to children's church. After church, Nick and I went to pick them up. As we were going down the stairs, I looked at Princess, and that little toot ***gave me the stink eyes AGAIN!!!*** Not good! As soon as we all piled into the car, I told the grandkids that as soon as we got home, they were to go directly to the kitchen table and chairs and sit down for the first "Anderson Family Pow Wow." Grampa happened to be home that Sunday, so I asked him if he would join us, and he did.

I prayed that God would give me the right words to say to these precious children. We had a serious talk about church behavior. When we are in God's house, we must be reverent and respectful of His presence there with us. I also addressed making stink eyes at me or anyone, for that matter. I told my grandkids how I expected them to behave in big church from then on.

The sweetest thing happened the next time the kids went to church with their dad and me. Every time the congregation stood up, Princess, who was on the other side of her dad, would jump right up and peer at me, smiling. Cam also stood up without being told to do so. After church, Princess asked me, "Gramma, did you see me stand up every time in big church?" I told her I did and that I was *so* proud of her and Cammie, too.

This was a conversation in the car on the way home from church another Sunday. Nick and I were in the front, and the kids were in the back. I overheard Cammie say, "Gramma, Princess said the F-word to me." Oh, dear. I turned around and saw Princess who looked like a rabbit with a gun to its head, so I knew she was guilty of something. I said, "Well, Cam, I guess you're going to have to tell Gramma what Princess said." He replied, "She said I farted." It's a good thing that Nick and I did not make eye contact! This was a teachable moment, though, so I turned around and said to Princess, "Oh, no, Princess. We do not say the F-word in this family. You can say, 'Cammie, you tooted,' or 'Cammie, you sputted.'" Nick and I had a big laugh when we got home. Kids! ☺

I love to go to Sunday school and "big church." It makes me sad to think of all the blessings, wonderful Sunday school lessons, fellowship with my Sunday school sisters, great sermons, and the awesome inspirational music that I missed all those years that I did not go. I learn so much, and I enjoy seeing my friends and fellow worshippers. Lessons and sermons that step on one's toes are so good for us. One of these days I may have to say aloud, "OUCH!"

My church has been so blessed to have had the same Minister of Music for over 30 years. Mickie is awesome! I look forward to the hymns we sing, the special music, and our phenomenal choir's message in song each Sunday. They absolutely lift me up every week. I take notes on the music as well as the sermons. Here are just a few:

From **Every Road**
*Lord, I give you every road, guide my steps and take control,
'til this journey takes me Home, Lord, I give you every road.*

Rachel Anderson

Lord, I give you all my past; help me to be free at last. . .

From **Whispered Prayers**
God is listening when we say them,
There is power in whispered prayers...

From **We Will Remember**
We will remember, we will remember,
We will remember the works of Thy hands,
And we will stop! And give you praise,
For great is Thy faithfulness.

Some more of my favorites are: **10,000 Reasons, Days of Elijah,** and **Great is the Lord Almighty.** We senior citizens always love to hear the old hymns like, **The Old Rugged Cross, Great is Thy Faithfulness, To God be the Glory,** etc. I know we all appreciate Mickie mixing the old with the new.

If you don't go to church, I hope that you will find one that fits your needs. Sunday school and church are good for our souls, and it makes our heavenly Father so happy to see us there. It feels so good to get one's spiritual battery recharged.

CHAPTER 6

Memoirs of a Daughter-in-law

L arry and his two siblings grew up in a small town in Oklahoma. His folks' names were Hubert and Jewell, but once the grandkids started arriving upon the scene, they were affectionately called MaMa and PaPa.

In 1968, I married Larry when I was 20, and he was 23. When he was honorably discharged from the Navy, we drove all the way from Washington, D.C. to Oklahoma. I was a Yankee, remember, and I had no clue where Oklahoma even was. When I looked it up on a map of the U.S., I could not believe that it didn't have an ocean! Crossing the border into Oklahoma, I was on the lookout for tornadoes and buffalo to stampede!

So many things were different in this foreign land: the food, accents, sayings, etc. I'd never heard of chicken-fried steak, chili and chili dogs, and of course, Frito pie. Gravy for breakfast? Gross! Except that it wasn't gross at all, it was delicious on MaMa's homemade biscuits. Okies had a twang when they talked, and I liked it. MaMa would tell me that something was "as flat as a flitter." I asked her one time what a flitter was, and she had no clue, just that she knew it was really flat. Okies use the word "fix" a lot. They fix their hair (is it broken, I wondered?), they fix dinner, and oh, sometimes they are fixing to fix something. I think the only thing New Englanders fixed were flat tires!

Larry and I went camping with MaMa and PaPa several times before we had kids. Talk about fun! Well, one day, the guys were fishing, and MaMa and I were in the camper "fixing" lunch. A song started playing on the radio, and I started laughing. I said, "MaMa, can you believe that song? Too funny!" Without missing a beat, MaMa sang along with the radio: "You get a line, and I'll get a pole, and we'll go down to the crawdad hole, Honey, oh baby, mine," and that sweet lady sang *all* the verses, too! We had a big laugh, and she answered my question as to what in the world was a crawdad.

We had a lot of fun trips and visits to their humble little two-bedroom home in Velma, Oklahoma. On one visit, I asked MaMa if Skeeter (Larry's childhood nickname) was spoiled as a child with his brother, Dwayne, 11 years older, and his sister, Barbara, 8 years older. She replied, "Oh, he was spoiled, but he didn't take to it." Didn't take to it???? He not only "took to it," he *loved* it! When Larry went off to college in Edmond, Oklahoma, to attend Central State College (later called Central State University, and now the University of Central Oklahoma), he talked MaMa and PaPa into moving into the Acacia frat house to be the house Mom and Pop. They lived in a little downstairs apt., so the spoiling continued. The only time that Larry wasn't spoiled was when he was serving his Naval Reserve active duty time; Uncle Sam does not spoil the troops! When we married, I took up the spoiling where MaMa had left off.

In July of 1985, 2 ½ years after losing MaMa to bone cancer at the age of 68, I attended a writing workshop for teachers in Abilene, Texas. I am including here a paper that I wrote for this course. Larry didn't read it until a couple of years before we lost him at 67 years old. He was sobbing. MaMa was loved and missed so much.

Memoirs of a Daughter-in-law

I'll never forget the first time I laid eyes on my beloved MaMa. I had already been married to her son for nearly three months. It was on a cool, autumn evening in October of 1968. MaMa and PaPa had driven nearly 1,600 miles from their home in Oklahoma to my sister-in-law's home in Virginia for this momentous encounter.

I was full of anxiety and anticipation as Larry and I pulled up to Barbara's home that evening. I'm sure that MaMa had been experiencing these same feelings and emotions as she appeared to be pacing back and forth on the front lawn. All my fears and worries vanished instantly as I hesitantly emerged from our car. MaMa came running across the lawn with outstretched arms and tears streaming down her face, smiling. The genuine warmth and all-encompassing love I felt in that first embrace will remain with me forever.

What a precious woman my mother-in-law was, always accepting people regardless of their race, creed, origin, or faults, forever seeing their good qualities and overlooking their flaws. One was always welcome in her humble home.

She was there to help me after the birth of both of my children. She adored her grandchildren, as they did her. She didn't shower them with material things, but she did with love, understanding, and support. She always found time for her grandkids, to listen to them, rock them, and get down on the floor to play with them. Her cookie jar was always brimming with her delicious, homemade goodies. She made our visits so special.

MaMa was our Rock of Gibraltar. She'd never been sick a day in her life, having had all three of her babies at home. She took pride in the astounding fact that at age sixty-seven she'd never had a prescription drug filled!

In March of 1982, MaMa complained of a pain in her right leg – nothing to worry about, probably old age creeping up on her. In June, on a visit to our home in Abilene, Texas, MaMa still complained about her leg. She had seen a doctor, though, and his diagnosis was arthritis. He prescribed Motrin (she pronounced it "Motrain") to relieve the pain.

In September, my sister-in-law, Barbara, telephoned me. MaMa and PaPa were in Houston visiting with her and her family. MaMa's leg wasn't any better. Barbara had her out walking every evening to exercise the soreness out of that leg.

A month later, in October of 1982, Barbara and her husband, R.A., drove up to MaMa's and PaPa's home in Velma, OK. This is when I began to suspect that something was not right. Barbara called when they returned to Houston. MaMa had really gone downhill since their visit one month previous. The pain in her right leg was worsening. Motrin was not helping. She was very obviously suffering. Arthritis, they said?

Larry and I had planned on having Thanksgiving dinner at our home that year. We called his folks. MaMa said they couldn't come. Her leg hurt too much to drive. PaPa was legally blind, and she had done all of the driving for many years. Something was wrong. Why wasn't her arthritis medicine working? How did she know that her leg wouldn't be better by then? It didn't make any sense to me.

So, Larry and I decided to bring the Thanksgiving dinner to MaMa. The shock I experienced upon seeing her on that somber visit shook me to the depths of my being. MaMa was sitting on the couch, so pale, so worn. She had always come out onto the porch to greet us whenever we had driven up their driveway on all of our numerous visits, so excited to see her loved ones. This wasn't like my MaMa at all. Something was terribly wrong.

MaMa sat there on the couch a very short time before she quietly uttered that she was tired and wished to lie down a while. One could have cut the tension in that room with a knife. She stood up very slowly, deliberately, grimacing all the while. To walk the short distance from the living room to her bedroom took several minutes. She was totally exhausted from the effort.

The look my husband and I exchanged was one of sheer panic. Larry adored his mother. He knew that I did, too. She wasn't just my mother-in-law, a relative inherited by the way of marriage. She had become my best confidante and friend. I loved her so much, and I needed her in my life.

My mind was racing. She was so ill, that was all too apparent. Should we ask her how she was feeling, how her leg was? It was so extremely obvious that she was in severe pain. Should we quiz PaPa? He looked frantic. What should we do?

Later that solemn Thanksgiving Day, MaMa courageously left her bed to come sit on the couch and sample my pecan pie – always striving to please, to pretend as if everything was all right. It was another pain-riddled endeavor to wend her way back to the living room, another exhausting journey. She heroically ate two bites. This was a woman with an appetite as big as her heart! Then it was back to her bed. This time she almost didn't make it. PaPa had to help her, to lie her down. It took another several heart-wrenching minutes to accomplish this task, the pain was so excruciating.

The phone rang. It was Barbara calling to wish us all a Happy Thanksgiving. I laid down on MaMa's bed as she conversed with her daughter. It was at that time I noticed congestion in her chest. Could MaMa have pneumonia? Is that what was wrong with her? As I laid there beside this woman whom I loved so dearly, my five-year-old son, Nicky, commenced to climb up on the bed to love on his grandma, too. Frantically, and with a firmness I'd never heard before, MaMa called out, "Don't touch my leg! Please don't hurt my leg!" I was fighting back the tears. Dear God, help her; help us all.

Before leaving, Larry and I made a decision. We would take matters into our own hands. We copied down the name of MaMa's doctor from her Motrin prescription bottle. We needed some answers and planned on calling the doctor the following day.

We didn't have to. PaPa called us. He was placing MaMa in the hospital the next morning for tests. He wanted some answers; so, did we.

That was the longest week of my life. The phone call finally came five days later on a chilly Saturday afternoon in early December. It was Larry's brother, Dwayne. My husband answered the phone. The look on his face was all I needed to convey the dreaded message – he could hardly verbalize the words: MaMa had cancer, bone cancer. He was sobbing uncontrollably. So was I.

My mind was surely playing tricks on me. They said it was arthritis! For nine months MaMa had been treated for arthritis, and all along she had bone cancer! We were in a state of shock.

Larry blindly threw some necessities into a suitcase. He was still crying. Our hearts were totally broken. Despair overtook our kindred souls. Then he was gone, winging his way to his beloved MaMa, and I was alone with my grief, fears, and panic.

Later that week, Larry came back home and drove the children and me to Oklahoma to see MaMa. She was in a small hospital in a nearby town adjacent to the one in which MaMa and PaPa lived. Larry cautioned me to prepare myself, to brace myself for the worst. MaMa looked dreadful, he said, and he admonished me not to break down and cry in her presence. We had to be strong for her; she needed our strength now.

As I walked down the corridor towards her room, I was screaming inside, "Don't cry! Don't cry! Be strong for MaMa!" The door opened at my beckoning. There she was, that once beautiful, silver-haired, blue-eyed, robust lady, now so pale, weak, and pain-racked, sitting up in a chair! She had her sons to put her there just for me. What a stoic! I embraced her gently, so fearful that I might cause her more pain. She smiled feebly, her voice low and shaky. I didn't stay long for she was exhausted from the strain. I had made it through that ordeal without crying, barely. My throat and head hurt so badly from holding back the flood welling up inside me. No sooner did I emerge from that room when I crumpled into a mass of unrestrained sobs. PaPa and Larry did, also. We bravely tried to comfort each other.

The little hospital in which MaMa had taken up residence was not equipped to handle cancer patients. The staff was doing all they could, but it wasn't enough. She simply lay there, languishing, for two weeks.

By then the family made a major decision. We had kept in touch with Barbara. She called M.D. Anderson, the world-renowned cancer institute in Houston, Texas. A specialist would see MaMa. The appointment was scheduled for 9 A.M., December 20th, 1982. MaMa's physician suggested that we transport her there in a van. A plane excursion, with all the moving and jostling, would be too painful for her. So, we organized a caravan. Dwayne would drive the van with Larry and PaPa tending to MaMa's needs. I would follow with our two little ones. We would gather up Dwayne's family in Dallas en route to Houston.

We left the hospital at midnight that cold, foggy, December evening. The scenario matched our spirits. Our nerves were frayed. Dear God, ease MaMa's pain. Keep me alert.

Every time the dome light in the van came on, my heart leaped into my throat. MaMa was heavily sedated. We had to make it to our destination! Perhaps chemotherapy would put this accursed disease in remission. Maybe we would have our dear, sweet MaMa back the way she was for at least a few more years. Barbara was already talking about purchasing a pretty silver wig for MaMa should her hair fall out due to the treatments and renting a hospital bed for the guest room. MaMa and PaPa would stay at her home to be close to the hospital. Our hopes were soaring now.

We pulled into Barbara's driveway at 7:30 A.M. We'd made it, fatigued both mentally and physically. I scrambled from the car and ran to the van, climbing inside to lie beside MaMa. She was awake. I held her wrinkled hand, so strong a year ago, strong enough to reel in a generous catfish, or open a stubborn jar of her homemade pickles, or throw a football to her only grandson. She smiled at me as always.

MaMa was admitted to M.D. Anderson that morning. She never again left that hospital alive, which was her secret fear and why, we learned later from a devastated PaPa, she had postponed checking into a hospital for so many months. I think she knew long before any of her family began to suspect the worst, that something was wrong, something more than merely arthritis. Maybe she did indeed feel that it was cancer.

Christmas of 1982 was a gloomy occasion, to say the least. It was spent around a hospital bed, trying to be cheerful, helping MaMa open her numerous gifts. I had bought her a beautiful silky gown and matching robe. They had lovely lavender flowers on a cream background. She never got to wear them.

We came home the following week, totally drained from the daily excursions to the hospital. Larry made numerous trips back to Houston in the ensuing weeks. I was teaching school and could not accompany him, much to my dismay.

At three o'clock on Friday afternoon, January 13th, 1983, the intercom in my classroom abruptly interrupted my thoughts. I hurried to the phone in the office, so fearful and assuming. It was Larry. MaMa had taken a turn for the worse. Barbara was calling all the family to come to Houston. I raced down the hall, blinded by the tears that were gushing from my eyes. My wonderful, compassionate colleagues were all gathered together in the hallway. I could not have told them what was wrong had they asked. They didn't have to; they knew.

The eight-hour trip back to Houston was a quiet one. The children didn't argue once, or even ask, "How many more towns, Daddy?" We were all deep within our own recesses, submerged in our thoughts and memories.

It was midnight when we pulled up to the curb in front of Barbara's home. The mood befit the evening of a month earlier when we ever so gently and lovingly placed our MaMa into the van. Everyone was there. We were the last to arrive. We spoke in hushed tones. Barbara filled us in on the hopeless details – MaMa had suffered complete kidney failure. She was in such torturous pain two days earlier that one could hear her screams far down the hall from her room. She was calling to her mother who died when MaMa was a teenager. She had lapsed into a coma, death's silent cousin.

We collapsed in bed at 2 A.M. that Saturday morning, only to be rudely awakened by the ringing of the telephone two hours later. It was M.D. Anderson. MaMa was in cardiac arrest. Come quickly! Help us, Lord! Help us all. Put Your arms around us.

We flew into our clothes. There were muffled sobs, worried looks exchanged. We piled into two automobiles with Barbara, her husband, R.A., and PaPa arriving first at the hospital. I saw them at the end of the hall outside of MaMa's room. PaPa was crying. Barbara was trying to console him, but in vain. I could see MaMa in her bed. The door was open. Her frail body was jerking erratically. Her eyes were glazed, staring straight ahead, seeing nothing. She didn't even know me.

We had to make another decision, the most devastating of all: to place MaMa on a life support system or not. This was unbelievable. The magnitude of this verdict was incomprehensible. Barbara solemnly asked the cancer specialist what MaMa's chances were. He quietly explained to us the rapid spread of MaMa's cancer. Her heart, lungs, liver, and kidneys were all involved now. She had no chance of survival. There really was not any decision to make at this point. The disease had already taken that option away.

MaMa's immediate family, PaPa, her two sons and daughter, couldn't bear to see her in her present state. Her mouth was curved downward. There were tubes coming from her mouth and nose. She had on an oxygen mask and catheter. She was hooked up to a heart monitor machine and blood pressure device. There was an I.V. needle in one arm. The tube in her mouth led to her stomach and blood was being pumped out into a sack to relieve the hemorrhaging there. Every three seconds she would gasp for air. I counted, thousands of times, and when she skipped a beat, my heart would lunge into my throat, fearing that the end had come. This sound was audible halfway down the hall. Her eyes were open and staring, yet there was no recognition there. Her hands and feet were a dark blue and so cold. It wasn't a pretty sight. My MaMa, my beautiful, silver-haired, blue-eyed, smiling, energetic MaMa. . .

What hurt me the most was the comatose state she was in when we arrived that morning. I couldn't converse with her. Many times I held her hand in mine those last hours and with a voice choked with emotion say, "MaMa, I love you. Please don't leave us."

At 1 A.M. the following day, Sunday, Dwayne and Larry took an exhausted PaPa back to Barbara's home. He looked a decade older than the 70 years he'd already amassed. God be with him. Comfort him. Barbara stayed at the hospital along with R.A. in the nearby waiting room, still not able to fortify herself enough to remain with her dear MaMa. So, Dwayne's wife, Barbara Sue, and I kept an all-night vigil.

I scooted a chair over to MaMa's bedside and held her hand. I laid my weary head down on her bed and closed my heavy eyes. She jerked so often and so violently that sleep would not come. I would try to rest a few minutes, then lift up my head and sob uncontrollably. I tried hard not to question my faith in God or His goodness and mercy. I guess He needed MaMa up in Heaven more than He thought we did. That was difficult to comprehend at best. At times I cried with frustration, "Dear God, let her live. Make her well. I *need* my MaMa! I can't give her up. Please?" At other times, after she'd had a seizure, I'd pray, "Lord, take her. Take her now. Please don't let her suffer anymore."

At 5 A.M., MaMa experienced a horrible seizure. She was jerking violently, gasping, hemorrhaging from her stomach. Blood vessels burst in her eyes. I thought she had died. Not having the presence of mind to ring for help, I ran to the nurses' station. Several nurses flew to MaMa's side. I was trying hard to get myself under control so that I could tell Barbara without being totally hysterical that her beloved mother was gone. Then I heard MaMa begin to breathe again! It couldn't be true! She was still hanging in there, fighting all the way. You trooper, MaMa! You never were one to give up without a fight. Remember when PaPa was fired early on in your marriage when you wrestled his boss's wife to the ground in the oil camp because she had boldly caught that wild turkey that *you* had been fattening up for weeks for *your* family's Thanksgiving dinner? PaPa lost his job, but you won the turkey! Oh, MaMa, I love you.

I closed her eyes. I couldn't bear to look at them after the hemorrhaging. I held her nearly lifeless hand in mine. Her face was etched in pain, even in her comatose state. At 7:30 A.M., my husband called. I picked up the phone by MaMa's bed, and with a trembling voice told Larry that the end was near, to stay home with PaPa. He said no, that he'd be on his way very soon. As I was about to hang up the receiver, I looked down at MaMa. The most peaceful expression spread across her face – a look I hadn't seen in months, and then with an enormous sigh, she was gone.

I'd never been to a funeral before. I was thirty-four years old. I'd never lost anyone remotely close to me throughout the years. Coming from a large family of six children and many relatives, I was always afraid that my first funeral would be that of someone I dearly loved. That fear materialized two days later as I sat at MaMa's funeral.

The morning MaMa passed away, our little family drove the eight hours back home in silence most of the way, too tired and drained to say much. The next day, Monday, January 16th, 1983, we drove the four hours to PaPa's home in Oklahoma to assist with the funeral arrangements. MaMa's body had been transported to the funeral home that day.

The women had decided to go to the funeral home first that evening. I'd never seen a deceased person before. When MaMa died the day before, I hurriedly left her room. Now I was to view her in her casket as she would appear at her service the following day.

As we walked into the sanctuary, I saw her at the end of the room. I gasped. She looked so real! Was she still alive? Maybe they'd made a horrible mistake! I stumbled towards her, stood beside the casket, and wept unashamedly. MaMa looked so pretty, so still, so peaceful. I watched her chest to see if it was moving. It wasn't. I picked up her hand. The warmth I'd felt in our first embrace was gone. On tiptoes, I kissed her cheek ever so gently, still fearful that

I might hurt her. Sobbing, I told her how much I loved her and said good-bye.

I had heard people say that time was a great healer of broken hearts, but I never really understood. Now I do. The first year without her was the most difficult. I'd be driving down a street and see an older couple out for a stroll, and I'd burst into tears. So many times, my memories of MaMa were tapped by some object, person, word, or phrase and I'd break down. I missed her so much. Letting go of someone I'd loved so intensely was hard.

A year and a half after my precious mother-in-law's passing (death, dead, dying – those words are still so difficult to write and say), my ten-year-old daughter, Buddy, came into the living room where her Daddy and I were sitting. She had her tape recorder with her. Buddy commenced to play a tape of Christmas, 1981, MaMa's last healthy Christmas with her family. I had forgotten all about that recording, but I knew what was coming: MaMa's voice with that sweet Oklahoma twang, describing in detail all the lovely Christmas gifts she had received that year. I thought I'd welcome hearing her voice. She didn't say but a few words when I burst into tears and had to leave the room. No, I wasn't ready. Perhaps someday. . .

Yes, I still grieve for my beloved MaMa, but it is with a sweet sorrow now. I have chosen not to remember her with sadness. MaMa would be fit to be tied if she got wind of that! I remember her with a joyful heart and cling to all of the wonderful, one-of-a-kind memories we made. Oh, I was selfish and wanted more, yes, but I have more than most. MaMa made my life richer just by *knowing* her, and I will forever cherish her memory and the lasting, indelible impression she made on my life.

The End

The year MaMa passed away, she and PaPa were to celebrate 50 years of marriage. PaPa cried for many months over losing his soulmate. Then he told us that one night, when he was in bed crying for MaMa, she appeared to him! She was dressed all in white, and there was this warm glow all around her. She told him that she was good and that she wanted him to be good, too. After that night, he was. God is SO good to us! That vision of MaMa was exactly what PaPa needed for his heart to heal.

This picture of our precious MaMa was taken in her last spring. When I look into her eyes, she has a distance in them that I had never seen before. I truly believe that she knew she was much sicker than she let on. She loved her family so much that she wanted our sense of normalcy to last as long as she could make it for us. MaMa left a legacy of love that still endures in our hearts after all these years. . .

CHAPTER 7

Doony

How could I possibly write this book without including a chapter on Doony, our beloved beagle? He was an important part of my life's journey for 12 priceless years.

I never had a pet before we got Doony. Larry had a sweet dog named Skipper when he was growing up. Our children, Buddy and Nick, really wanted a puppy to love. Buddy would beg for one, pleading, "I'll never ask for another birthday or Christmas present. I will feed the puppy, walk him, and give him baths. I'll never ask for anything ever again if I can just have a puppy. Pleeeease?" Well, she finally wore her dad and me down, so we started looking for a puppy in earnest.

It was 1984, and we were still living in Abilene. Buddy was 10, and Nick was 6 ½ years old. One day we saw an ad in the local paper: "Beagle Puppies for Sale." I'd always thought that beagles were so cute, and so did the family. We made an appointment to go look at the pups.

Oh, what an exciting day that was for the Anderson family! There were lots of beagle puppies in that litter, and they were all running around their owners' garage for us to observe. One little beagle puppy came over to Larry and started chewing on his tennis shoes' laces. We took that as our sign. ☺ Doony was 6 weeks old when we brought him home that day. Our lives would never be the same.

I knew absolutely nothing about dogs, beagles in particular. Beagles are hounds with a very keen sense of smell. They are bolters, running off chasing scents, and they are very fast, too! Doony didn't bolt very often while we lived in Abilene. I think that was because we had a wooden fence, and he couldn't see all the activity on the other side. Once we moved to Granbury, he bolted every chance he got!

I can't remember how old Doony was when I enrolled him in Obedience School. He was probably a year old. When I would put Doony in the van to go to the vet's, he was everywhere, jumping from seat to seat! It's a wonder I didn't have a skillion wrecks with that hyper pet going wild. When I would take him for his walk around the neighborhood, he was pulling *so hard* on his leash that it was a chore for me to try to get him under control. I knew that we had to do something, so off to Obedience School we went.

The sessions were held in an elementary school gymnasium. I remember the first day we arrived. Doony, of course, was jumping all around the van, as usual, on our way there. I put his leash on him when we got out of the car. Doony was lunging and pulling me behind him. Phew! We got inside, and he was still out of control. All the while, he is baying, "Awoooooooo! Awoooooooo!" like hound dogs do. We got to the gym and went inside. The trainer was there and several other pet owners. These people were standing next to their pets who were behaving perfectly, sitting beside each one. When Doony and I came bursting into the gym, and Doony was howling for all he was worth, they were grabbing up their pets! I mean really! I was thinking, "What on earth are these people doing here? Their pets are so good and obviously well-trained already. I'm here with Doony because he is out of control!"

We got through all of the sessions, and it did help. Doony learned how to "sit" well, for about 5 seconds, but hey, it was an improvement! He also learned to, "stay" for maybe 3 seconds. The big difference was when we would go for our walk. He did not pull me like he used to do. He still wanted to sniff everything along our way, but when I pulled on the leash, he would come with me.

When Doony was 4 years old in 1988, we moved to Granbury. We had our builder put in a doggie door for Doony. He didn't have one in Abilene, so Buddy had to show him how to use it by crawling through it. Doony loved it and the freedom it allowed him. The doggie door came into the heated and air-conditioned utility room where his water and food bowls were as was his bed. Doony's bed was under a built-in table, so it was really cozy under there for him. He even had his very own log cabin dog size quilt that I custom made for him. He was definitely spoiled with lots of love from his family, and we were totally loved by that precious pet in return.

Not long after we moved, Doony was due for a checkup with our new vet. As I was paying the bill afterwards with Doony on his leash beside me, one of the receptionists called Doony a dog!!! I had to explain to her that Doony did not know that he was a d-o-g! Bless his heart! I hoped that experience didn't scar him for the rest of his life. ☹

We had decided to have a chain link fence installed when we built our home so that Doony could see what was going on around him. He loved it! There was one drawback, though. Since Doony could see now, he became a digger! He would dig out from under the fence and take off! Several days when I would come home from school, I could see Doony lying on the sidewalk in front of our home, waiting for me. He couldn't get back into the yard. We were warned by Security that if Doony got out again, we'd be looking at a $200 fine! Ouch! So, we decided to put up an "electric" fence all around the chain link fence. The first time that Doony got zapped, he squealed and ran back into the utility room for safety. We felt badly, but we really didn't have much of a choice. Doony quit digging, and all was well.

One Halloween about 9 P.M., Doony was outside in the back yard just barking away. We were getting ready for bed. I remarked to Larry that the trick-or-treaters were gone, so Doony couldn't be barking at them. He decided to go outside and see what was the matter with the beagle. It wasn't long when I heard Larry and Doony in the kitchen. Larry had the dry heaves; Doony had been sprayed by a skunk!!! The skunk aroma one smells from a considerable distance away is nothing like it is up close and personal. It is gut-wrenching alright! Larry was in no shape to take care of the situation, so I grabbed Doony and got him into the tub. I'd never heard of using tomato juice on skunk spray before, so all I could think of to do was to shampoo that poor pet. I think I shampooed him at least 3 times; the smell was still so bad. I didn't know what else to do for Doony, so I put him to bed. It took several days for the skunk stink to go away.

Doony's favorite treats were popcorn and pizza crusts. One evening, we were sitting at the kitchen table eating pizza. Of course, Doony could smell it in his "dog cave," so he slid his two front paws under the utility room door. I called this action, "Two paws under the door." Buddy grabbed one of the crusts and went over to the paws. She got down onto the floor and slowly slid the crust closer and closer towards Doony. We saw his tongue, and all of a sudden swoosh! Doony had sucked that pizza crust out of sight! We heard his doggie door as he went outside. Talk about funny! Doony came to the glass patio door. The pizza crust was stuck to his teeth! He looked like the Joker on Batman with this huge grin. We laughed and laughed. The pizza slice would not come off until it softened in a few minutes. This picture has been on our fridge for many years.

When Nick was in middle school, the fundraiser that year was selling summer sausages, cheeses, etc. He came home from going door-to-door one day and put a lone sausage on top of the washing machine. Lo and behold, the next day, the sausage roll was gone! Nick *knew* he had put the sausage there the day before. We looked all around – no sausage, so he had to pay for another one. Months went by, and one day when we were out back, guess what we found? The sausage wrapper! I could just imagine Doony in the utility room jumping up as high as he could over and over again until finally the sausage was within his reach. We hoped he had enjoyed his feast!

Larry took Doony for his walk every morning, and I did after school. One year I bought a bright red sweater for him to wear on cold days because I was afraid that he might be chilly. He was stylin', let me tell you! ☺

When Doony was 10 years old, he developed some heart problems. Trips to the vet became more frequent.

In June of 1996, Larry and I drove Nick to the airport to board a plane for the Air Force Academy in Colorado Springs, CO. There would be NO contact with our son for 6 weeks! That was tough. We remembered how sad we were when Buddy left home for the University of North Texas, 62 miles away. Nick was the "baby," and he was going far away. We remarked on the drive home that at least we still had Doony. Seeing Larry crying in Nick's room later that day broke my heart. . .

Three months later in September of 1996, Doony's heart condition worsened. When I came home from school one day, Doony could not get up. I carried him to the car and cried all the way to the vet's, crying some more over his fur on the examining table. They told me that he would have to spend the night there again like he had a few times in the last year. Every other time I picked him up the following day, so when I left home for school the next morning, I laid Doony's leash on the front seat, ready to grab when I picked him up that afternoon.

For some reason, I decided to go to the Teachers' Lounge mid-morning and call the animal hospital to see how Doony was doing. I can still hear the receptionist's voice saying: "We tried to reach you before you left for school; Doony's heart gave out this morning, and he died." I don't remember anything else she said. I was sobbing so hard. I knew I couldn't stay and teach, so I got a sub and went home to grieve. It took me a very long time to stop crying. When Larry came home and saw me in the kitchen, he knew. We hugged each other for a long time and cried together.

I had to go to school the next day; there is no time off to grieve for a beloved pet. With God's help, I made it through that first day, and I didn't start crying until I got to the back door. The following day, I made it to my car, then out of the parking lot, then home before I had a meltdown.

One of the hardest things for Larry and me to watch was the slow disappearance of the little trail Doony had made from 8 years of walking along that path from his doggie door to the patio. We missed everything about him. For days, I swore I heard his dog tags jingling from his collar when he'd walk or run.

Before we got Doony, I could never understand how pet owners could go on about their frou-frou dogs, the Fifi's and Puddin' Pies, etc. Then Doony came into our lives. A pet is definitely an integral, important member of one's family.

Doony gave us so many happy memories and his unconditional love. We were so blessed to have had that beloved beagle for 12 years. Garth Brook's song, "The Dance" makes me think of Doony sometimes. If we'd never had Doony join our little family, we would have missed the pain of losing him, but oh, we would have missed "the dance" as well.

CHAPTER 8

Work Ethic

I was blessed to have parents who had strong work ethics. My dad was in the Air Force for 30 years. During this time, he also worked many Saturdays at Edie's Apple Orchard to bring home extra income in helping to raise six kids. Dad planted and maintained a large vegetable garden for our family. Ma would can lots of vegetables for the winter months.

Mothers rarely worked outside of the home during the 50's when I was growing up. Ma kept a spotless home, sewed many of our clothes, and served delicious meals (well, maybe not liver & onions – YUK!) for our family. Every Saturday morning, Ma would give us kids our lists of chores to do before we could go outside to play. I swore that she laid awake nights thinking up those chores! We had to have had the cleanest baseboards in town! Ma had a saying about our efforts: "If you're not going to do a job right, don't do it at all." One year, when I was teaching 5th grade, I told my class what Ma said to my siblings and me. One of my students said, "Well, then I wouldn't do it at all!" Hello! I told him that one had to read between the lines back then and figure out what our parents were really saying. What Ma meant was that if you didn't do it right the first time, you *would* be doing it again. I remember this kid looking at me like, "Huh?"

Some of my happiest memories are the first years of our marriage when we were really poor. I worked in a bank to put Larry through grad school, and then he taught school and coached to put me through school. Three months after we were married, we moved to Oklahoma with very little to our names. We borrowed MaMa and PaPa's rollaway bed because we couldn't afford to buy our own. This contraption folded up in the middle and had a latch to keep it shut when not in use. The mattress had seen better days as it was pretty old and well worn. In the middle of it was this valley. Larry and I would roll into each other when we climbed in to get a good night's rest. Not! So, we fixed the problem by stacking some old Life magazines underneath that cavernous midsection. Voila! Problem solved! ☺

We played cards with friends for free entertainment and ate "tube steak," quite often, Larry's name for hot dogs. I drove MaMa and PaPa's old Impala that was like 20 feet long, and Larry drove an old, white, beat-up truck with holes in the floorboard (really!). He called it a "semi-automatic" as the gear shift would automatically shift from 1st to 2nd. I went to the Laundromat the first 5 years of our marriage until we were finally able to buy a mismatched secondhand washer and dryer. I was 5 months pregnant with Buddy, and I felt like a Queen! To this day, I love my utility room and washer and dryer. Going without and saving our money to purchase what we needed or wanted made us really appreciate them more.

During my years of teaching 3rd grade at Dyess Elementary in Abilene, Texas, I went through a phase where I did not want to work. My kids were one and four years old. I remember having similar feelings when Buddy was an infant, too. Picking up those "lumps of sugar," as MaMa called them, from their cribs, having to wake them up, get them both dressed and fed, diaper bag ready, and both dropped off at the nursery, was exhausting. I was pooped by the time I got to school! I wanted to be a stay-at-home mom and be with my little ones. I had to give myself an AA: Attitude Adjustment. I knew that if I didn't work alongside of my husband (so to speak) to help support our family and save money for our kids' college educations, we would struggle. The kids would have to take out mega college loans to go to college. I knew that I needed to work, so I had an epiphany: you can work and be miserable, or you can work and have a good attitude and love what you do for a living. That did it. I chose to really enjoy my job, which I did love, and not look back on any unhealthy wishful thinking. It made a huge difference in my life.

In October of Buddy's senior year of high school, she was accepted to attend the University of North Texas. That same month, her dad lost his job. He had worked for 16 years in sales. The company was "down-sizing," and thousands were let go. Larry took a humble pill, fell back on his teaching certificate, and taught and coached in a junior high school, which was what he did right out of college, 23 years earlier. He worked his way up to teaching and being on the coaching staff of the Granbury Pirates football team when Nick was a junior and senior there – what a gift for both of them! Larry eventually ended up in administration. The Master's degree he earned all those years ago paid off.

I would tell my students that work is good for us. It gives us a sense of accomplishment, especially when we take pride in our work by doing our best. I would also tell them that work comes before play. On Saturdays during the school year, I would have loved to sit down and quilt on my latest project, but I had a house to clean, laundry to do, grocery shopping and other errands to run. When I laid my head down at night, if I didn't have any time to quilt, I felt good about taking care of my family.

I remember my folks saying to us, "We can't afford it." I'm glad they did. It taught us to find ways to earn money, save it, and then we could purchase what we wanted.

Nick came up with a spreadsheet of Cam and Princess's chores when they were little. On "Payday" he would tally up their totals every week and pay them accordingly. ☺

Camden		Monday	Tuesday	Wednesday	Thursday	Friday	Saturday	Sunday	Total
	Make Bed	$0.05	$0.05	$0.05	$0.05	$0.05	$0.05	$0.05	
	Put Things Away	$0.05	$0.05	$0.05	$0.05	$0.05	$0.05	$0.05	
	Eat What Was Given	$0.05	$0.05	$0.05	$0.05	$0.05	$0.05	$0.05	
	Homework	$0.05	$0.05	$0.05	$0.05	$0.05	$0.05	$0.05	
	Brush Teeth	$0.05	$0.05	$0.05	$0.05	$0.05	$0.05	$0.05	
	Table Manners	$0.05	$0.05	$0.05	$0.05	$0.05	$0.05	$0.05	
	Stick/Pecan Patrol	$0.05	$0.05	$0.05	$0.05	$0.05	$0.05	$0.05	
	No Fighting/Hurting	$0.05	$0.05	$0.05	$0.05	$0.05	$0.05	$0.05	
	Be Respectful	$0.05	$0.05	$0.05	$0.05	$0.05	$0.05	$0.05	
	Good School Morning	$0.05	$0.05	$0.05	$0.05	$0.05	$0.05	$0.05	
	Behave in Church							$0.05	
	Total								
Sydney									
	Make Bed	$0.05	$0.05	$0.05	$0.05	$0.05	$0.05	$0.05	
	Put Things Away	$0.05	$0.05	$0.05	$0.05	$0.05	$0.05	$0.05	
	Eat What Was Given	$0.05	$0.05	$0.05	$0.05	$0.05	$0.05	$0.05	
	Homework	$0.05	$0.05	$0.05	$0.05	$0.05	$0.05	$0.05	
	Brush Teeth	$0.05	$0.05	$0.05	$0.05	$0.05	$0.05	$0.05	
	Table Manners	$0.05	$0.05	$0.05	$0.05	$0.05	$0.05	$0.05	
	Stick/Pecan Patrol	$0.05	$0.05	$0.05	$0.05	$0.05	$0.05	$0.05	
	No Fighting/Hurting	$0.05	$0.05	$0.05	$0.05	$0.05	$0.05	$0.05	
	Be Respectful	$0.05	$0.05	$0.05	$0.05	$0.05	$0.05	$0.05	
	Good School Morning	$0.05	$0.05	$0.05	$0.05	$0.05	$0.05	$0.05	
	Behave in Church							$0.05	
	Total								

Proverbs 28:19 - "Work brings prosperity; playing around brings poverty."

CHAPTER 9

Teacher Tales & Tips

Psalm 32:8 - "I will instruct you (says the Lord) and guide you along the best pathway for your life; I will advise you and watch your progress."

When I was little, I wanted to be a cowgirl when I grew up. When I rode my first horse on a family vacation in Colorado, I realized that I was scared to death of horses, so being a cowgirl was not going to work out for me. I also thought about being a nurse, something I would have loved, but I have fainted at the sight of blood more than once in my life, so that was out as well.

After I married and decided to go back to school and get my degree, I hoped I would become a mother someday. The thought of my little ones spending their summers in daycare while I worked was troubling me, so I thought about majoring in elementary education. I would be off virtually every day the kids would be, and also, I loved children, so this was a no-brainer. I thank God for calling me to be a teacher.

During my senior year at Central State University (now the University of Central Oklahoma), I did my student teaching in a 4th grade classroom in Edmond, OK. I will never, ever forget my awesome cooperating teacher, Freda Hunt. She was the epitome of an elementary school teacher. I used many of her methods during my whole 32 years of teaching. After graduating in 1972, I taught 6th grade that first year in El Reno, Oklahoma. My principal, cohorts, and students were wonderful. Since I taught in a different school district than Larry and commuted 30 miles each way, I decided to try to land a teaching position in Larry's district. I was hired to teach 3rd/4th in an open concept school. Again, the Lord blessed me with another wonderful principal, teachers, and students. In the middle of my third year there, Larry decided to change professions and go into sales with a company where several friends and former educators/coaches worked. We packed up our little family (Baby Buddy was 22 months old) and moved to Abilene, Texas, in January of 1976.

In 1977, our son, Nick, was born. I started substitute teaching for Abilene ISD when Nicky was 6 weeks old. That was one of the hardest things I have ever done. If it hadn't been for my dear neighbor, Jane Bell, taking care of the baby during this time, I don't think I could have ever left him then. Subbing paid off, and in the spring of 1978, I was hired to teach at Dyess Elementary School and finish out the year for a 1st grade teacher who moved. A 3rd grade teacher was retiring that year, and I jumped at the chance to teach 3rd grade. I have taught all grades from 1st-6th, but 3rd and 4th are my favorite grades to teach.

I taught 3rd grade at Dyess Elementary the next 10 years of my career. My four cohorts, or "cohearts" as I call them, awesome veterans, took me under their wings and taught me what teaching was all about. All of them, Mickie, Mary Nell, Barbara, and Shirley, were very dedicated, knowledgeable professionals. They shared everything with me, including how to teach cursive writing, my favorite subject to teach. The kids are SO excited about it, and every child can succeed. It grieves my soul that cursive writing is not being taught anymore in most school districts. I am SO happy that I saved my wonderful Palmer cursive writing manual/lesson plans; I simply could not part with these treasures. The Lord knew I needed to keep them because my BFF teacher friend, Marsh, decided to change grades last fall and teach 3rd grade. She used my cherished Palmer materials and taught her class how to write in cursive 1st semester! Yeah! I am so proud of her and her students. What a gift this is to her class!

A funny story happened when I first started teaching at Dyess. In Social Studies we were learning all about Texas: the state flower, bird, and song, the capitol, etc. This was "back in the day" when teachers ate lunch with their kids in the school cafeteria. We sat together at the teachers' table. Our principal, Elmon Higgs, one of the best, would sometimes sit and have lunch with the teachers. He was having lunch with us third grade teachers that day. The first 4th grade teacher, Valeta Wicker, to come to lunch sat at the table with us, too. I was telling everybody how much I (a transplanted Yankee) was enjoying teaching my class about Texas history and learning along with them. I told them I loved the state song of Texas and that I remembered learning and singing this with my mother when I was little, growing up in New England. Valeta had her suspicions, so she asked me what the state song of Texas was. I proudly replied, "Why, The Yellow Rose of Texas!" Valeta commenced to correct me saying, *"That's not the state song of Texas! Everybody knows the state song of Texas..."* blah, blah, blah.... All the while, I am *mortified* because this happened in front of my principal!!! I wanted to say, "Well, thank you very much, Valeta," but I didn't. I did say to her, "Well, what *is* the state song of Texas then?" to which *she* proudly replied, "The Eyes of Texas are Upon You!" (which is the school spirit song of the University of Texas!) Oh, the look on Elmon's face...priceless (the state song is "Texas, Our Texas"). ☺

When autos came equipped with cassette/CD players, I would play music on the way to school that would get the juices flowing, like Bob Seger's "Old Time Rock 'n' Roll," or Elvis's "You Ain't Nothin' but a Hound Dog." On the way home was a different story: a little Kenny G or B.B. King to unwind with . . . ahhhhh...

Teacher evaluations began during my tenure at Dyess. Our principals would come into our classrooms, sit and observe us teaching, all the while writing down notes on evaluation forms. These were very stressful events for us teachers. I think we had like 45 points to cover during our 45-minute lesson. Hello! We could barely *think* much less remember all of those! Talk about stressful!

One Friday in October, I had planned on having my class make witch faces in art. I was short one sheet of 12x18 "witch face green" construction paper. So, I thought I would just mosey on over to 2nd grade teacher Nelda Turner's room across the hall to see if she had one I could have. I must tell you here that I am very unobservant. I saw Nelda standing in front of her class teaching away. She was dressed like she might be going to church after school. I mean, she looked really nice that day! I remember standing in her doorway trying to get her attention; she would not look my way! I think I either knocked or said, "Mrs. Turner? Would you happen to have any light green construction paper that I could borrow?" She kind of had on a crabby face as she waved me in and pointed to her shelves along the opposite wall. I'm thinking, "Well, excuuuuse me!" So I slinked (slunked?) behind her and found the construction paper. I had to squat down and go through several packages before I found what I needed. Slinking back to her hall door, I stopped to thank her. She *still* would not look at me! So, I said, "Thank you, Mrs. Turner." Nelda just kind of rudely waved me away, like communicating to me to shoo!

After school that day, who should come to my room but Nelda and her coheart, Dena. Nelda asked, "Do you have *any idea* what you did today?" I'm thinking *hunh*??? Come to find out, Nelda was being evaluated by our principal, Don Rogers, who was sitting at a little table like 5? 6? feet away from me as I was pawing through Nelda's paper!!! He witnessed the whole fiasco! No wonder Nelda was taken aback by my intrusion. I was so embarrassed, to say the least, and very apologetic. The good sport that she always was, we had a big laugh, *and*, after that episode, teachers actually put up signs on their doors the day of their evaluations that said, "Mrs. Anderson, Do Not Enter!" How rude! ☺

I remember after an evaluation lesson of mine, Mr. Rogers left a sweet note on my desk. I filed it in my Sentimental File. It's notes of appreciation like my awesome principal wrote that day that encouraged me and spurred me on for months.

In the spring of 1988 Larry got transferred from Abilene to Granbury, Texas. My last day at Dyess Elementary, I cried all the way down the hall after picking up my last paycheck in the office. I don't remember if I was even able to talk to or hug my dear 3rd grade teacher friends. That was a very sad day for me.

From 1988-2006, I taught elementary school in Granbury: thirteen years in 4th grade, one in 2nd, two in 5th, and two teaching 504/ESL students. Once again, God blessed me with wonderful principals and cohearts. During those years, I had the awesome privilege to mentor some of the finest first-year teachers on the planet: Melinda, Cheryl, and Marsh, to name a few. They had a knack for teaching and a deep love for their students and their jobs. They all taught me so much, as did many, many more phenomenal teachers the Lord put along my pathway. One of the biggest blessings of my life was mentoring Marsh who became my dear friend. We have so much in common: 2 children (both of us have sons named Nick), we love teaching, we are hand-quilters, and we're both Christians. God is good, so good!

Sentimental File

All during those many years of teaching elementary school, I kept a Sentimental File which ended up becoming two folders. I saved many precious notes and papers from my students, their parents, fellow teachers, and administrators. These treasures fuel us teachers on for months. I've been retired 14 years now (where *did* the time go?), and every once in a while, I will sit down and reread those priceless items. I would like to share a few with you here.

When I taught 3rd grade at Dyess, one year I had this little boy who had many problems concerning academics and behavior. His name was Walter. Only two students in my 32 years of teaching, had to have their desks right next to mine as they could not function sitting close to their peers. One day, after dismissing my 3rd graders, I walked back into my classroom, and there on my desk was a folded piece of 3rd grade handwriting paper from a Big Chief tablet (I am looking at it right now). On the front it said: "to: Mrs Anderson from: Walter." I opened it and read, "deer Mrs Anderson I love you. And I know you love me too." It made me cry, for sure. Here was this little guy, whom I had to put my thumb on constantly every day, yet he still loved me, and most importantly, he knew that I did indeed love him, too. Wow – how special is this note that I have kept over 30 years.

The other student who had to have his desk right next to mine was Jason. He had lots of problems, too. I was teaching 4th grade here in Granbury. Since 4th graders had to take the state's writing exam every spring, I wanted my kids to have lots of writing practice, so each day I had a sentence starter for a paragraph on the board. One day the starter said, "I would like a magic ring that..." Jason finished the sentence with "would change people into a frog. Or that made money. Or it made cars. Or made houses. Or made me have Mrs. Anderson for a teacher every year. That would be fun. Because she's the nicest prityest coolest Teacher in the World!" So dear!

This paragraph Jason wrote in the spring. The starter was: "The best time for me is when..." Jason finished that sentence and paragraph with this: "...I get to go to Mrs. Anderson's class (he went to a special class during part of the day). I like it there. Mrs. Anderson is nice to the class when they behave. But if you don't behave you'll get in big trouble. Like a tan rear end and a note home. She might be strickt but she's still nice. So don't act dumb and act up. Because she'll paddle you herself. But she's still the Best Teacher in the world. The End."

Just a little footnote here about Jason. The first 3 days of school I had to take him to the principal's office, he was so disruptive and disrespectful. One of the best principal's I ever had was Billy Jack (love these southern names) Henderson. He was so supportive of us teachers. Jason learned that Mr. Henderson and I meant business when it came to discipline. When we were making our 3rd trip to see the principal in 3 days, I told Jason, "Young man, you have met a brick wall named Mrs. Anderson. I will not tolerate disrespect and neither will Mr. Henderson." I guess that 3rd trip made a believer out of him because it was our last one. I was so proud of Jason's turn around. He and Walter both will always have a special place in my heart.

Set the Stage

I've always felt that kids needed parameters, and actually, they **wanted** them, even if they wouldn't admit it. I would ask my students, "How many of you were in a loud, rowdy classroom last year?" Years ago when I would ask that question, only one or two hands went up, but over the years, so many kids raised their hands. I would see some of them with their hands up looking at friends with their hands raised, shaking their heads affirmatively and grinning. Like that was a good thing? Hello! Then I would say, "It's not like that in Mrs. Anderson's room." The hands went down *so* fast, and I'm sure those students hoped I wouldn't remember who raised their hands. It actually tickled me, but I kept a straight face. I know that my students appreciated knowing that I expected them to behave in school, and they did!

The Hokey Pokey

Another thing I did on the first day of school was to play the Hokey Pokey with them at the end of the day. Well! Some of my kiddoes would not participate, especially some of the boys. They'd look at each other with an expression of disgust; after all, they were big 4th graders now. The rest of us had a big time! I had a CD of music with songs, "Big Band Hokey Pokey", "Hokey Pokey Rock," etc. Talk about fun! When we were through, I told the class that I was going to hand out their *first* Homework Pass of the year. These were few and far between and highly sought after. Only the students who **participated** in the Hokey Pokey would receive one. The looks on those faces of the hold-outs was priceless. It didn't take too many days before one of them would start asking me, "Can we do the Hokey Pokey today, Mrs. Anderson?" Lesson learned. ☺

First Day of School Parent Letter
And Responsibility Pie Graph

The first day of school I sent a personal letter home with my students for their parents to read. In it I told them a little bit about myself, like where I was from, went to college, a little about my family. I closed my beginning of school letter with these words of wisdom: "If you will believe half of what your child tells you about school, I will believe half of what he/she tells me about home." ☺

The first day of school is SO important as it sets the tone for the rest of the year. During our talks, I would draw a pie graph on the board labeled, "The Pie Graph of Responsibility." There were 3 sections: one was labeled "Student," one was "Teacher," and the 3rd section was "Parents." The "Teacher" section was bigger than the "Parents," but not by much, and the "Student" section was by far the biggest. We talked about this. I told them that in order for them to have a good year in school, each of us three had to take our responsibility seriously. If we did, they would succeed.

Bullying

During the school year, something would happen, most likely on the playground, where a child got his/her feelings hurt due to harsh words. I told the kids that old saying, "Sticks and stones may break my bones, but words will never hurt me," was so not true. It should say, "Sticks and stones may break my bones, but words can break my heart." We would have a good discussion concerning bullying, something I would not tolerate, ever! I wanted my kiddoes to feel safe in my classroom, on the playground, in the cafeteria, on the school bus, everywhere concerning school. I would ask my students what they thought the #1 reason was that kept kids from telling their teachers about being bullied. It was always the same answer: fear of retaliation. My kids were also afraid to tell us teachers things for fear that we would think they were tattling. We would have a discussion about the difference between tattling and telling a teacher, parent, etc. something very important for them to know. I told them that we can't help them if we don't know what is going on.

I'll never forget one year when some of my kids told me that a 6th grade boy was taking my little Ashley's lunch money, like every day! Grrrrrrrr! I told my students on the first day of school that I was like a mother grizzly, and they were my cubs. I got the kids busy and then went down the 6th grade hall and found this young man. His teacher let me take him out into the hall. We were nose-to-nose when I told him that I knew all about him taking my Ashley's lunch money. I made it clear that she was not the one who told me, also. I told him that he **would** repay her what he owed her, apologize to her, and promise never to do something like this ever again! Then I asked him if he knew what the word "retaliation" meant. He said he did. I told him if he thought I was upset now, it wouldn't light a candle to what would happen to him if he **did** try to get even with my student.

(I hope this chapter doesn't sound like rambling, but I really want to share some teaching tips that may help others besides teachers, so please bear with me.)

Students' Precious Gifts

Over my many years of teaching elementary school, I have received some sweet gifts from my students. "Freshly picked" flowers sometimes came from yards other than theirs! They knew I loved rocks and had a rock garden at my home, so they would bring me interesting rocks from family vacations, etc. One year, my little Shelby brought me a pretty necklace made from pop beads (remember them?) that she had designed herself. If I remember correctly, some were little, and some were quite large. I wore it with pride all day. Well, I had to run to the grocery store after school. When I was standing in line to check out, I felt eyes on me. I knew something was amiss, but what? Perhaps I had "playground duty hair?" It wasn't until I looked in the mirror when I got home that I noticed those sweet beads. ☺

Another year when I had to make a grocery store run after school, I felt eyes on me again. Did I have a piece of spinach in my teeth? I was in the produce department when I saw my reflection. I was still wearing a large fuchsia-colored plume clipped to my hair, another precious gift from a sweet student.

Valta Heffley*, a wonderful 4th grade teacher at my school, was coming up the hall with her kids on their way to lunch one time. I was walking towards her having just dropped my kiddoes off in the cafeteria. It was Valentine's Day, and Mrs. Heffley was wearing a crown that one of her sweet students had made for her from some manila paper. On it were these words: "Queen of Heats." Thank the Lord we didn't get tickled right then because this was a precious, handmade gift from one of her little girls. Valta wore that crown with pride all day long, not thinking for a second that it may have smushed her hair, etc. I think she still had it on during bus duty after school, too! ☺

*In loving memory: 9/17/1936 – 10/1/2017

Reading to the Class

Every day when we would come in from recess after lunch, I would read to the class. Kids who needed to finish assignments could do so while I read, sitting on the bar stool. Sometimes I would read a 20 minutes book like Chris Van Allsburg's, **The Widow's Broom** (oooohhhh! So good on Halloween!). During the year, I would read many chapter books such as **The Hundred Dresses, Mom, You're Fired!, The Adventures of Tom Sawyer** (The chapter, "Tragedy in the Graveyard" is the *best!*), **Helen Keller, Robinson Crusoe, The Best Christmas Pageant Ever**, etc. The best days were when I would stop at a "cliffhanger." The kids would say, "Noooooooooo!" They were so into our book. I saved my favorite chapter book for the last 8-10 weeks of school, **Summer of the Monkeys**. I read this book to nearly 30 classes, and every year I would cry at the end. They were happy tears, but I just couldn't help myself. One year my little Amber got up and brought me a tissue. Too sweet! So many times, whether it was when we were lining up to come in from recess, or when we got back to class, one of my kiddoes, even the boys, would ask, "Are you going to read to us, Mrs. Anderson?" They loved this time as much as I did.

Science and Social Studies Baseball

Our science and social studies tests were *hard*! Since they were part of the curriculum, we had one at the end of every chapter. The class knew when these tests would be, and so did their parents as my kids had a calendar with important information like this written down. Even with studying, it was still hard for the kids to succeed. So, I came up with Science or Social Studies Baseball. The class would be divided into two teams. I named them the first time we played: The Fritos and The Cheetos. ☺ Then I designated where the bases were. A Frito would come up to home plate, and I would ask him/her a question with multiple choice answers. If the Frito got the answer right, he/she would advance to first base, and a teammate would then be up. If kids got the answer wrong, they would have to sit down, and this would be an out. Three outs and it would be the Cheetos' turn. When we would play Baseball at the beginning of the year, the kids did not realize that I was using the actual test questions and answers! We didn't have enough time to get through all of the questions. Since we covered the chapters in class, and the tests were difficult, IF they really listened during the game, they would pass the test.

Barnyard!

Every year, most times only once, I would play "Barnyard" with my kids on a Friday at the end of the day. I would warn the other teachers near me because they knew we would be loud. You may want to do this with your class or some of you at a party, reunion, etc. Here's how you play "Barnyard." I would tell my kids that we were going to play a fun game called "Barnyard." First, I would walk around the room whispering the name of a barnyard animal in their ears. There was no talking during this game except when they made their noises (you don't want them to tell each other their animal due to Round 3). There would be more than one of each, 3? 4? So I would whisper, "Pig," "Rooster," "Horse," "Donkey," etc., ***but NO cows***, not until the 3rd round. Okay, so after I had whispered in everyone's ear, then I would say something like this: "You all know that we do not get loud in our classroom, but when we play Barnyard, we do. So, when I say, 'One, two, three, GO!' make the noise of your barnyard animal. I am listening to see what group, say the pigs, turkeys, whatever, is the loudest. When I make the cut sign, stop immediately. Got it? Okay, but wait until I say the whole count, 'One, two, three, GO!'" When I did, they were oinking, crowing, braying, etc., etc. Then I would make my stop sign, and they did. I told them that it sounded to me like the donkeys were the loudest, so they won Round 1. The donkeys were grinning and so proud. I told them that we needed to do this again and not let those donkeys win twice. I also told them that if I gave them the same animal as in Round 1, they could whisper that to me, and I would give them a new one. So I repeated what we did, but this time I said I thought they could do better. You're really getting them into this. Oh, and this is SO important! Be watching in Rounds 1 & 2 for a kid who is really getting involved. After Round 2, declare the winners, could be those Roosters, and brag on everyone. Tell the class we will do this one more time, and *this* time the winning animals will receive homework passes! Yeah!!!!! Okay, so you go around the room one more time, but *this* time you whisper, "Don't say anything," in everyone's ear except for the kid who was really getting into playing Barnyard. In his or her ear, you whisper, "Cow." Tell the class you want the principal to hear them in her office this time! When you say, "One, Two..." the cow is inhaling. HA! And when you say, "Go!" get ready for the loudest, longest MOOOOOOOO! Ever! My kids would fall out of their seats they were laughing so hard. The "Cow" laughs, too, especially since they get that Homework Pass. We all leave the room that day on a laughter high. ☺

I was reading through my Sentimental Files recently, and I came across a sweet letter my student, Jeff, wrote to me over 20 years ago. In part, he wrote: "I also loved all the games we played, my personal favorite was barnyard. The way you tricked all of us by telling everybody to say nothing, then getting the new kid." What he meant by getting the new kid was if we got a new kid (and we must have the year I taught Jeff) I swear their first day, someone would ask if we could play barnyard with him! Poor thing! I always made us wait at least two weeks so we wouldn't run off our new student their first day!

I think we played Barnyard virtually every year I taught because I learned how to play this when I was living with my sisters in New Hampshire. We went to a "Tupperware Party," and the hostess introduced us to this game. The winner would receive (and she held it up for all to see and covet) this lovely set of bowls for the prize. Well! When we got to Round 3 and the hostess starting counting, "One, Two..." my sister, Joyce, was inhaling!!!!! Her face bright red and her, "Mooooooooo!" lasted several seconds before she realized that no one else had made a sound. Way too funny! I went to an assembly at the high school during our son, Nick's, senior year. Dusty, one of my 4th graders who was now close to graduating, too, came up to me and told me that he would never forget being the cow in barnyard. I told him that he was a Barnyard Hall of Famer! I can still see and hear him mooing. ☺

A couple of years ago, I ran into Christa, one of my 2nd graders from the only year I taught 2nd grade in 1993-94. We hadn't seen each other in many years. She said to me, "I remember being the *only one* who said, "MOOOOOOOOOOO!" in Barnyard. Oh, how well I can recall her cow, also! Christa definitely deserves to be in the "Barnyard Hall of Fame," too. ☺ I just hope that I haven't scarred these precious "cows" for life!

Do the Right Thing Banner

For many years, I displayed a banner above the cursive alphabet in the front of our classroom. I made the letters out of bright neon green poster board and mounted them onto a black background. The poster, more like a large sentence strip, said **Do the Right Thing.** I talked to my classes about the importance of what those words meant. I told them about something that had happened to me many years ago. I had to go to the bank to get some cash one day. The drive-through teller gave me the amount I requested, or so I thought. I pulled up so that customers behind me could take care of their transactions and also so that I could count my money. The teller had given me an extra hundred-dollar bill! Having been a teller before, I knew how important it was to balance one's window at the end of the day. I worried about what might happen to her when she came up short $100. That extra bill was like a hot potato in my hand! No way would I have kept it because I knew that it would have been the worst hundred dollars I'd ever spend. The Lord would have punished me big time, so I drove around to the front of the bank, walked in, and gave the teller back the hundred-dollar bill. The look of gratitude on her face was SO worth it.

Many times during the year something would happen, and I would point to that poster. School isn't just about academics. It's also about learning lessons that stay with our students all of their lives.

The Wheel of Good Behavior

Many years ago, I was fortunate to attend a wonderful seminar concerning classroom management. One of the presenters was a man who taught special education. He told us about the Wheel of Good Behavior. I came up with my own wheel to fit in with my classes. The "Wheel" was a big circle cut out of poster board. I divided it into several sections such as: School Supply (new pencil, eraser, etc.), Homework Pass, Aggie Kickball, and Lunch with Your Teacher. That section, if you can call it that, was *exactly* on a line. ☺ In the middle of our wheel, I attached a spinner using a brad.

When my class received 20 **unsolicited** compliments, we would get to spin the Wheel of Good Behavior. Wow! Most of our compliments came when my class was walking down the halls to lunch, P.E., etc. When I did my student teaching, I learned from the best, Mrs. Hunt, my cooperating teacher. She had "3 Rules" when the kids lined up and walked down the halls: face the front, hands and feet to yourselves, and no talking. I learned over the years to inspect what I expected, too, so I would turn around every once in a while, to check up on them. They were SO good! When passing a teacher or our principal, they might say, "Oh, my, what a wonderful line you have, Mrs. Anderson!" I got to brag on my kiddoes then. If you brag on your kids in front of others, they work even harder to live up to your expectations. The funny thing is that when they would receive a compliment, all 22 hands shot up because each of them wanted to be the one to put up another tally mark beside our wheel.

By far, their favorite thing to win was Aggie Kickball. We would head out to the playground during the afternoon to play. In Aggie Kickball, the kids had to run the bases backwards. Sometimes one would forget, and it looked like the Keystone Cops out there running into each other! Too funny! If the teams were even, I was their cheerleader. I remembered 2 cheers from our son, Nick's, Peewee Football days. The little cheerleaders for his team would say these cheers: "We're A-W-E, we're S-O-M-E, We're awesome, we're awesome, To-Tal-Ly!" I would add to this cheer, "Rah! Rah! Rah! Go, team!" Or I would do the cheer: "We are loud, and we are cocky. We'll run over you like a Kawasaki! Un-huh, yeah, yeah, yeah...un-huh, yeah, yeah, yeah." Then more Rahs and Rahs. Aren't you impressed out there in reader land? I told the kids that they would have to look very closely when I did my jump because it was like an inch off the ground and very fast, too. Now if the teams were uneven, oh, dear, I would have to play. How I pitied the team who got Mrs. Anderson! Bless their hearts. Let's just say that I am athletically challenged, and leave it at that.

Smileys ☺

When I would grade my students' daily assignments every evening, I had a stack of stickers beside me. I put one on papers 80 and above, and on papers such as handwriting that showed me one's best effort. I also drew Smileys on the 80s and above. I made a Smiley Chart that hung on my wall with amounts and prizes. My students would cut out the Smileys from the graded papers I sent home each week in the Red Folders on Thursdays. They couldn't do this until Mother and Daddy saw their papers. They would save their Smileys and cash them in when they wanted something from the Smiley Chart. 30 Smileys might be a new pencil or eraser top, 100 might be a Homework Pass, and so on. 250 was a pizza party at lunch for the host and 3 of their friends.

When my students were seniors here in town, some of them would send me a graduation announcement. I would send them a card with some cold, hard cash (☺), and I always tried to write a memory about them when they were in my class. Some of them sent me the sweetest thank you notes *ever*. I remember two of my girls reminiscing about Smileys. One still had many in her dresser drawer, and she wanted to include them in her card, but Mother didn't think that was a good idea, so she went ahead and drew all of them for me on the back. Too dear! The other student included a few with her note. ☺

Hobbies

I tried to impress upon my students how important it was for them to have a hobby. Hobbies help us to pass time, whether it is to rest and relax, or maybe to have something to do while we have to wait for someone or something. Perhaps collecting coins, sports cards, or learning how to embroider, knit, or sew would be fun for some of them. I need to have hobbies that produce something with my hands, so I piece and hand quilt quilts, knit, embroider, do counted cross-stitch, needlepoint, etc. I suggest reading, cooking, gardening, getting involved with 4H, whatever one enjoys. I can honestly say that I am *never* bored; there are not enough hours in the day for me to accomplish everything that I want to do. Just keeping up with the yard work and housework keeps me busy, but I need my "hobby time," to unwind.

Jobs

Every Monday morning, I would assign jobs. It was important to be sure that every student had a job to do for the week. Here are most of them:

Line Leader: I went in alphabetical order. The Line Leader was first in line. I always put my arm around the shoulder of my Line Leader, and we would walk down the halls together. Only one student in 32 years sort of bristled the first time I hugged him, so I didn't do that with him.

<u>Door Holder:</u> This child was second in line. He or she would hold doors open for the class, like when we would come back inside from recess.

<u>Energy Manager:</u> He/she was last in line, and their job was to be sure that our classroom's lights had been turned off when we left our room and that our door was closed.

<u>Computer Assistants:</u> This was important and such a big help to me. We had 4 computers in our room, and two students' jobs were to uncover them each morning and boot them up. At the end of the day, they would shut them down and recover them.

<u>Policemen:</u> I assigned 2 Policemen to report our class's behavior at lunch. Since I wasn't there with them, I wanted to be sure that they were held accountable for their actions. We went out to recess right after lunch, so when we came back to class, I would say, "Police Report?" Rarely was a student's name brought up. If one was, I would have the class vote as to whether or not this student needed to "sign the book." The vast majority of the time, the student in question was let off the hook. Kids are so sweet! IF the vote did not go in their favor, I would give that child a choice: either sign the book (we called these "marks," and they went home each week on their behavior card for their parents to see and sign –yikes!) or stand on the wall outside during recess. 100% chose to miss recess. Boy, I would have, that's for sure!

<u>Errands Runner:</u> What a big help my Errands Runners were to me! I might need them to take something to the office, or need my water bottle refilled, or the office might need something from me, and Errands Runner could deliver it. The list goes on!

<u>Paper People:</u> I arranged my classroom in groups of 4 desks, sometimes 5, etc. Every week at each group I would assign one Paper

Person to collect papers for me. They needed to have them face up, all going the same way, etc. They were awesome!

Classroom Monitor: I came up with this job when I happened to be in the little hall outside of the office where the intercom was located. The secretary buzzed a class asking for the teacher. I swear every child answered her, and they were SO loud and rowdy! Oh, my! I thought, I hope *my* kiddoes don't do that when I'm not there! So, each Monday morning I assigned one student, and only one, to politely answer the intercom should I not be there. They were also the one to report this to me in case I didn't know.

Board Eraser: This one makes me sad as classrooms don't have chalkboards anymore; they have dry erase boards instead. When we had chalkboards, Board Eraser would erase what I needed them to erase at the end of the day, and also they would take the erasers outside and "clap" them clean.

I'm sure there were other jobs, but everyone had this one. About 5 minutes before dismissal, I would say, "Hit the deck!" Every child had to get down and pick up all the specks from the floor around their area. They would signal me to inspect when they thought that their area was "speckless." The group with the cleanest area got to go out to their lockers first. My last year of teaching, I noticed that Mason was picking up "specks" all during the day, and he had his group do the same. Smart kid because his group was practically always first to go out to their lockers having a speckless area! Once in a while I would catch kids throwing their trash under a neighboring group's area. I made them retrieve their trash and told them if that happened again, they would be cleaning that group's specks for a week. It never happened twice.☺ I would tell my kiddoes about hitting the deck the first day of school, letting them know that our mess was not the janitor's mess to clean up. We were responsible for that. The janitor told us our room was the cleanest in the whole school. My kids were so proud, as they should have been. What a big help they were to me, too!

Portraits

Every May I would have my kids draw me. I always saved lots of fun things to do the last month of school to hold their attention and keep my sanity. I wish I had told my students to be sure to write their first **and** last names on the backs of their pictures and also the year. Some of these renditions are 40 years old, and I cannot remember all of their names and the years. ☹

Drawing by Cy Sonderer

I instructed my classes to draw me with their 12x18 inch piece of manila paper turned the tall way. I told them to just draw me from the waist or shoulders up. This way my face would be more visible (I was brave!). When they tried to draw all of me, those early pictures ended up with me being very small, and there was too much background. I would tell the kids not to forget the background, though. One student drew mountains behind me! Too cute! Some would draw me sitting at my desk, or standing by the chalkboard, etc. I knew I was in trouble portrait-wise when a student told me he was having a hard time drawing my head, so could he use my coffee can/pencil holder to trace for my face? Oh, my! It was round, all right. ☺

Drawing by Courtney (Coker) Godding

I laminated these portraits every year and would rotate them out in the hall by my classroom door. I had enough to change these keepsakes each week. Oh, the grins from my cohearts – priceless. There was the coffee can face one, and only one student over the years turned her paper the wide way; I swear I looked just like "Pat" on Saturday Night Live! These portraits are such treasures to me that I brought them all home when I retired nearly 14 years ago. I pull one out when Marsh comes to visit and tape it to the glass storm door. I keep encouraging her to do this with her classes. I hope some of you do, too.

Bingo

It was a rare treat when my kids would get to play Bingo with me. This game actually is great to play at class parties, like the Christmas party, because the kids are super excited on party days, and keeping them under control is not easy. Think about it, though; Bingo is a quiet game! Yeah! They love to play, and they are quiet because they really have to listen. Well, we would play games like Regular Bingo, Double Bingo, 4-Squares, etc. I always felt sorry for the kids who had cards that weren't so great, so I came up with Stinky Card. I would tell them that we were going to play Stinky Card. They all had to stand up. When I called a number on their cards, they had to sit down. The last one standing had the stinkiest card, and they won! Yahooo! My grandkids, Cam & Princess, almost always choose to play Stinky Card when it is their turn to name the game. I think they do this because Stinky Card is pretty fast, and they get to go to the prize table more often if they win. ☺

Art

At the beginning of each school year, I would tell my students that if we worked hard to learn our lessons during the week, we would get to have art on Fridays. They loved this, and so did I. I had a huge Art File of original ideas, but many were precious ideas shared with me by awesome teachers over the years. I loved displaying my kids' art work all around my room and sometimes in the hall. They were happy to see their efforts in finished form, and it gave them a sense of ownership. This was their classroom decorated with their art. It made our classroom special.

Show and Tell

I could probably write a book about Show and Tell. It was one of the highlights of my week. I saved this for the last 15-20 minutes of the day on Fridays. We would have Shows first since those kids brought something from home, and if we had time, which we usually did, we'd have Tells. I did this most of my career, and I did it mainly for one reason. I was very shy as a kid. I wanted my little shy ones to be brave and participate in Show and Tell when and if they were ready to do so. I had the kids sit on the bar stool at the front of the room. Sometimes, a child had an "assistant." ☺ Towards the end of my teaching, I found this neat sign that lit up, blinking, and had sound. The sign read, "Applause!" and you heard clapping and cheering. My kids would clap and get so excited. One of my students each week got to be in charge of the Applause sign. I will share a few Shows and Tells with you.

When I taught 3rd grade at Dyess Elementary in Abilene, one of my little girls had a Show to share with us (her mother was an awesome aide at our school). I wish I could remember this little girl's name. She went up to the bar stool and proceeded to take several little bottles out of a sack. She then held each one up and showed us how pretty they all were. These were liquor bottles that Momma had saved over the years from flights she had taken!!! When I saw her mom after school and told her what her daughter's Show and Tell was that Friday, she was mortified, having no idea that this was her little girl's Show and Tell! Mom asked me, "You did notice that none of them had ever been opened, right???" We had a big laugh. ☺

I remember Mutaga's "Tell" one year while teaching 3rd grade at Dyess. Once in a while, a kid would tell a joke. This is one of the reasons why I taught elementary school – because I am so elementary! Mutaga's joke made me laugh out loud, as did the class. At the supper table that night, I told his joke to the kids and their dad: "What's yellow and goes up and down?" "A banana in an elevator!" Haaaaaaaaa! ☺ Buddy, Nick, and I laughed, for sure, but Larry just sat there staring at us. How could he keep a straight face? That joke was funnnyyyy!

Another time, one of my little girls, Lenzi, came into our classroom that Friday hauling a big, black trash bag behind her. I knew whatever was inside had to be heavy because Lenzi couldn't carry it, and she was all sweaty from the exertion! When items couldn't fit into my students' desks, they would put them on the floor behind my desk and filing cabinet so their classmates couldn't see them before time. I helped Lenzi drag the bag behind my desk. When it was time for Show and Tell, she and her assistant carried the bag to the front of the room. They took the surprise out of the bag and set it on the bar stool. It was a huge wild boar's head, stuffed and mounted to a wooden base for displaying! When placed onto the stool, the head faced upwards, and those huge fangs jutted out. It was really scary looking. We called him Spike. Lenzi's grandpa (I believe) had caught that thing years earlier, and he had written down some information concerning the boar on an index card. Lenzi shared that with us. The kids were so impressed with her Show and Tell! Well, after school, I helped her carry that dude down the hall to the display case where her grandma was sitting, waiting for her. She asked Lenzi what was in the bag, and Lenzi showed her. Her grandma had no idea that Lenzi had brought Spike to school for Show and Tell!

A few months before retiring, I had a Show and Tell. Once in a while I participated, too. So, this Friday, I had my assistant close the blinds as I turned off the lights. Then I sat on the bar stool and told my class that I had just bought a new watch at our local Wal-Mart; my old one had bit the dust. I couldn't wait to share with them this awesome feature – my new watch had a built-in nightlight! A nightlight! I pressed the face on my $25 Timex watch, and on the light came, so bright and cool! All of a sudden, several of my kiddoes held up *their* watches with similar nightlight features, and they turned theirs on, too! Man! These kids were 10-year olds. I was 58. So much for my last Show and Tell... ☹ ☺

Sub Folder
A.M./P.M. Folders
Lesson Plans

Having subbed in Abilene made me very well aware of how hard this job was. I wrote my lesson plans with subs in mind: I didn't want them to be really wordy (subs don't have that much time to read), nor did I want them to just say "Page 25." I wrote my daily plans on cards that I had printed at a local print shop. There were lines for the subject, page(s), assignment, and then the procedure. These cards were about the size of an index card. Each subject had their own "stack" of cards. I had them written for the whole year after finishing the first year of a new manual/book. The beauty of these cards was that if we didn't get to that day's lesson (due to an assembly, etc.), the card stayed on top. When I taught that lesson, the card was put on the bottom.

All of each day's worksheets, etc., were ready to go in my A.M. & P.M. daily folders: Monday A.M., Monday P.M.," etc. My lesson plans stated where to find them. I never left school without being prepared for the next 5 days at least.

I kept a "Sub Folder" on my desk in plain view. It told my sub about my plans and where to find everything, like teachers' manuals, etc. I had the names of 2 students who would be great helpers to them, and also the names of nearby teachers who would be awesome help as well. I had my Daily Schedule, Duties, Procedures, etc., in that file. Should my subs need this, I had extra activities for the kids to do to keep them busy and quiet, like word searches, coloring sheets, etc.

I thanked my subs and told them I had subbed myself and that I really appreciated their hard work. I also asked them to please leave my room the way they found it, and to leave me a note concerning the kids' behavior, naming names if they needed to do so. I really can't remember a sub ever leaving me a bad note! My kids knew what I expected of them should I have to have a sub, which was rare. They were so good. ☺

The Good Citizens' Workshop

When I taught at "Old Intermediate" here in Granbury, teachers there had bus duty after school from like 2:45 – 4:00! Phew! After a long day of teaching, a lengthy bus duty wasn't easy. One Friday, two boys in either 5th or 6th grade, were very disrespectful to me just as their bus was coming. I can't remember what they did or said, but it was bad. I told them to meet me in the principal's office at 8:00 the following Monday morning and not to be late; they did not want me to come looking for them. I was very upset with the way they treated me.

I was stewing about this that weekend when suddenly I had an epiphany. Would having the boys see the principal teach them about respect? No, it wouldn't. I believe the Holy Spirit was speaking to me, and He helped me to come up with this mini course on respectfulness. I sat down and wrote out a weeklong, 5-day set of plans. I needed a name for this, and when I told my husband, Larry, about it, he said, "Why not name it "The Good Citizens' Workshop?"" I *loved* that, so I did.

I am enclosing my "Good Citizens' Workshop" for you teachers, parents, grandparents, etc. The "Copyright: 1992" is not official, just the year I came up with this. I will explain a few things to my teacher readers should you choose to use this. I believe it really helped my attendees to work on being more respectful.

This workshop took place after school for the whole week. I kept my "clients" for about 30-45 minutes is all, but I needed their parents' permission, and also if necessary, the kids would need a ride home.

The essays each attendee wrote were awesome. What a difference a week of attending The Good Citizens' Workshop made in them! I was SO proud of them and their progress.

Page 7, the "Respect Receipt," states that 10 different people had to sign this form, and 5 had to be adults. Well! Some of my "graduates" had signatures that looked like scribbles. When I asked who and how old the person was who say signed line 5, I heard things like, "My sister, Susie, who is 2 years old, did." Oh, give me a break! Like Susie would really see a difference in her older sibling's respectfulness. So, I had to tell them that I expected them to use their common sense, etc., and to only have people sign their form who could vouch for them. When they had their 10 acceptable signatures, and they returned the form, they earned a Coke and a candy bar from the Teachers' Lounge! Woohoo! ☺

I'm not sure how many students attended my respect workshop the last 14 years of my career. There probably weren't even a dozen, but I can say this – every single parent gave their permission to let their child attend. Wow! How awesome is that? Some parents even wrote me notes thanking me for doing this. I was so impressed with their willingness to want their child to become more respectful. We are all in this education business together.

One year I was asked to present my workshop to a group of teachers at another campus. For several years when the attendees came into my classroom after school, I would play Aretha Franklin's hit, "R-E-S-P-E-C-T," on the record player with my "Aretha's 30 Greatest Hits" LP. I know, most of my millennial readers have no clue what an old vinyl LP was. This song really got the kids fired up, and me, too! I knew that year that I would be driving to a school across town for my presentation, so I left the LP in my car. DUH! The LP was vinyl!! AND, it was practically a triple digit day!!! When I reached to retrieve my treasure, it had melted into a scary blob! I was heartbroken. We didn't have Google, Amazon, etc. back then, so I thought I could try to sing it, or spare them. Good for them I chose the latter. ☺

GOOD CITIZENS' WORKSHOP

By Rachel Anderson*

Rachel Anderson

_____
Date

Dear _____,

_____will be attending my "Good
Citizens' Workshop" the week of _____
because _____
_____
_____
_____
_____
_____
_____
_____
_____
_____
_____
_____
_____
_____
_____
_____
_____
_____

Thank you for your support.

Sincerely,

_____

The Good Citizens' Workshop: Lesson plans for a 5-day mini-workshop in respectfulness.

<u>Day 1:</u>

Discuss the definitions of the word *respect*. Write them on the board/overhead (including this one: "to show thoughtful consideration for others"):

<u>Respect</u> (ri spekt) V. 1. to feel or show honor or esteem for. 2. to show consideration for: *I will respect my teachers*. N. 1. consideration. 2. regard. 3. courtesy: *The respect she showed her parents was wonderful*.

Write on the board/overhead, and discuss the following words:

1. <u>honor:</u> high regard or respect; adherence to the principles considered right; integrity.
2. <u>esteem:</u> to value highly; respect – to consider.
3. <u>consideration:</u> thoughtful regard for others.
4. <u>principles:</u> rules of conduct.
5. <u>conduct:</u> behavior.
6. <u>integrity:</u> honesty; sincerity.
7. <u>courtesy:</u> good manners, kindness, politeness.
8. <u>regard:</u> a favorable opinion; appreciation.

Hand out index cards and have student(s) copy this definition:

"Respect: to show thoughtful consideration for others." Write this definition a total of 5 times.

Take the definition home and memorize the meaning of respect. Be prepared to recite the definition tomorrow.

Day 2:

Ask participant(s) for the definition of respect: *"to show thoughtful consideration for others."* Praise!

Brainstorm about how one shows disrespect. List ways on the board (including the following), and discuss as you go:

1. rolling one's eyes.
2. pulling away from an adult.
3. answering "Yeah," "Yes," "Nah," or "No," instead of "Yes, ma'am," and "No, sir," etc.
4. making a face.
5. making a face at a person behind his/her back.
6. making an obscene gesture.
7. being dishonest.
8. vandalizing.
9. muttering under one's breath.
10. having the last word.
11. being inconsiderate.
12. arguing.
13. having rude manners (burping, etc.).
14. being sarcastic.
15. talking ugly.
16. disobeying.
17. being defiant (*boldly resisting authority"*).
18. breaking rules or laws.
19. glaring.

Have the student(s) recite the definition of respect with you: "Respect means: *to show thoughtful* consideration *for others.*"

Day 3:

Recite the definition of respect with the student(s):
"Respect means to show thoughtful consideration for others."

Brainstorm – How do we show respect? List ways on the board/ overhead, discussing as you go. Include the following:

1. having an acceptable look on one's face.
2. by not pulling away from an adult.
3. saying, "Yes, sir," and "Yes, ma'am," etc.
4. by always telling the truth.
5. being considerate of others and their property.
6. doing what you are told and doing so the *first* time.
7. no muttering under your breath.
8. not trying to have the last word.
9. never arguing.
10. by always using your best manners.
11. being obedient.
12. being punctual.
13. by treating others the way you wish to be treated.
14. by not swearing.

Ask: *"Why should we show respect?"*

1. It makes us feel good inside.
2. It makes others feel good about themselves.
3. <u>It is the right thing to do.</u>

ALWAYS DO THE RIGHT THING!

<u>Day 4:</u>

Ask: "Who can give me the definition of respect?" (*Respect means to show thoughtful consideration for others.*") Praise!

Ask: "Whom should we respect?" Brainstorm, making a list on the board/overhead (include the following):

1. our elders (explain who our *"elders"* are!)
2. our parents, step-parents.
3. our brothers, sisters, step-brothers, & step-sisters
4. our grandparents, aunts, uncles, & cousins
5. our teachers, principals, secretaries, aides, student teachers, etc.
6. cafeteria workers
7. referees
8. our neighbors
9. policemen
10. our President
11. our friends
12. our classmates
13. bus drivers
14. custodians
15. clerks
16. aides
17.
18.
19.
20. *Everyone!*

Note: In today's lesson, a student usually brings up the fact that some people do not deserve respect, such as drug dealers, mean, dishonest, rude people, etc. This is a good time to explain that yes, respect must be earned.

Repeat together: "Respect means to show thoughtful consideration for others."

Day 5:

Write an essay entitled:

"What I Have Learned About Respect"

_____

_____

_____

_____

_____

_____

_____

_____

_____

_____

_____

Name _____

Date _____

(This essay is due the next school day.)

Rachel Anderson

Respect Receipt

I have seen an improvement in _____'s
respectfulness and behavior.

Signed	Position	Date

Turn in this form when complete but not sooner than two weeks from
today. Ten (10) different signatures (5 must be adults, and 3 of those
5 must work at this school!) entitles _____
_____ to _____
_____.

Way to go, _____!

Good Citizen's Honor Roll

<u>Name</u>   <u>Date</u>

_____

_____

_____

_____

_____

_____

_____

_____

_____

_____

Upon completing The Good Citizen's Workshop, I gave certificates to the participants. There are many on the internet, and homemade ones are always great, too. I'm sure the attendees and their parents were proud of them.

Teaching school is a job with lots of responsibilities to our students, their parents, our administrators, and the district. Doing one's best by them, giving 110%, whatever it takes to help your kids to be successful is so rewarding. Make school fun, but let your students know that learning their lessons is #1. Love them, encourage them, brag on them. I truly believe that *all* of my students were handpicked for me by God. I was so blessed.

The first year I retired I went through withdrawal from teaching. The first day of school that fall was very difficult for me. When that big, yellow school bus came rumbling up my street, it made me so sad. For the first time in 32 years of teaching, I didn't have my own class. I also felt like I had lost part of my identity: I wasn't an elementary school teacher any longer.

Before you know it, dear teachers reading this, your careers will end, too. Make the most of each and every day. I had this note on my desk towards the end of my career: "Rest is sweet when one has earned it."

Colossians 3: 23-25 – "Work hard and cheerfully at all you do, just as though you were working for the Lord... remembering that it is the Lord Christ who is going to pay you, giving you your full portion of all He owns. He is the one you are really working for..."

Okay, so I *thought* I was done with this chapter, but then I was talking with my big sister, Joyce, and she asked me if I had included the following stories about John and phonics. When I said no, she pleaded with me to please do so. They are endearing, so here goes:

I only taught 2nd grade one year. What a precious class God gave me! John was just an adorable student. Well, one day when our 2nd grade classes were outside enjoying recess, I heard John coming; he was crying. As he approached me, he cried, "Jimmy hit me with a blade of grass. . . A BLADE OF GRASS!" And in between 2 little fingers was the evidence - the actual blade itself. My 2nd grade cohearts had to turn around so as not to get tickled because this was a serious situation, mind you. Jimmy was also in my class that year, and he and John did not get along. So, I had a talk with the boys, hoping that their relationship would improve soon afterwards.

One morning I was teaching John's reading group phonics, the two sounds of "o-w." I had a phonics wheel. The "ow" remained the same, but the beginning sounds changed when I would move the wheel. The children were supposed to read and recite their word, then say what one of the 2 sounds of "o-w" the word made, such as, "snow / o," or "plow / ow." When it was John's turn, he only read and recited the word "cow." We kept waiting for him to tell us what sound the o-w said in his word. We waited and waited until I finally said, "and it says???" John made this disgusted sigh (like as old as you are, Mrs. Anderson, and you don't know???), and in a big voice blurted out, "MOOOOOOOOOOOOO!" The whole class erupted in laughter, including me. John looked so surprised, and I thought he might cry, so I took him out into the hall and loved on him, explaining that we weren't laughing at him, it was the funny mooooo. ☺

When I was teaching my 2nd graders that year the 3 sounds of "a," as in cat, ape, and ball, I told them there was a 4th sound when a person is from New England, like their teacher was. That sound is "ah," like in the words calm (cahm), bath (bahth), laugh (lahf), etc. Well! My 2nd graders, try as they might, could not say that 4th sound of "a," it always came out as "aw." I had to go to the doctor after school soon afterwards, and when the doctor said, "Stick out your tongue, and say, "Ahhh," I thought, that's it! This is universal! Everyone says, "Ahhhh," when their doctor tells them to do so! I was so excited when I was teaching phonics the next day, telling the kids that they *could* say the 4th sound of "a" after all. I told them about my doctor's visit the day before and said, "When the doctor tells you to stick out your tongue, you say…???" and in unison, the class said, "AWWWWWW!" That's those precious Texas kids for you. A Yankee teacher teaching phonics to children in the South can be a real challenge some days.

I promise this IS the end of "Teacher Tales and Tips." ☺

CHAPTER 10

Get Out of Jail Free

I like to read Dear Abby when I have time. Several years ago, I read her column about a highway patrolman who pulled someone over, I think for speeding. When he asked the perpetrator for her license, she also handed him a "Get out of Jail Free" card from a Monopoly game. He thought that was so funny; I decided to put one in my purse, as well.

In all the years that I have been driving, I can only think of 3 times that I have been pulled over by a policeman. One of those times was when I was heading back to my campus after attending a meeting at the high school. I barely started down the highway when I saw a police car behind me with its lights on. The policeman was motioning for *me* to pull over! I couldn't believe it. The first words out of my mouth were, "Officer, I promise that I was not speeding!" thinking that had to be the reason why he pulled me over. He said, "Ma'am, you weren't speeding, but the sticker on your license plate has expired." I said, "What? I have no idea what you mean by that because my husband takes care of that stuff. Man!" I should have zipped my lips right then and there, but oh, no, I had to continue with, "Don't you get a new one at the same time you get your car inspected?" The officer said, "No, ma'am, this sticker here..." he went to show me where the inspection sticker was on the front windshield... "has expired, too." I couldn't believe my luck.

He started writing me *two* tickets when I remembered Dear Abby's column, so I retrieved my "Get Out of Jail Free" card and handed it to the Officer. He laughed and laughed, so much so that he tore up one of the tickets giving me a warning instead.

I still had the other ticket to take care of, so I went to see the Judge. I spoke with his secretary first and handed her my ticket *with* my card. She started laughing and walked into the Judge's office. I could hear them both heehawing in there. I still had to pay for the ticket, but we all had some good laughs that day.

I know I gave my husband, Larry, one of these cards, and I think I did Buddy and Nick, also. Nick's family Monopoly game was missing lots of pieces, so he was going to throw it away, but not before I found the two "Get Out of Jail Free" cards. I have them saved for my 2 grandkids, Cam and Princess. I'm going to laminate them and put them in their 16th Birthday cards. ☺

CHAPTER 11

Guardian Angel Alert! Angels, too

Psalm 91:11 - "For He orders His angels to protect you wherever you go."

As long as I can remember, I have always been a climber. I think we either are or are not. My daughter wasn't a climber, but my son was one from the day he learned to crawl. He crawled to the couch, pulled himself up, and then hiked a chubby leg up onto the couch and tried to climb up! He was a climber from that day forward.

At 5'3" and shrinking (5'2" at my last doctor's visit – yikes!), I still hop up onto counters and stand on them when I need to reach something in a tall cabinet. About 12 years ago, I climbed up onto the clothes dryer in the utility room because I needed to get some yarn on a top shelf. Unbeknownst to me, I had my heels planted firmly on the dryer door. All of a sudden, it sprung open, and down I went hard onto the floor. I broke my left leg. One has to do what one has to do when one is vertically challenged!

Several years ago, when we still had 3 tall yaupon holly trees across the front of the house, I would climb up our 6' ladder with the electric clippers. I had to stand on the next to the top step holding the electric clippers in one hand and grabbing onto the yaupon for dear life with the other as I tried to reach as far as I could to trim that thing. My arm would get so tired holding those heavy clippers. I nearly fell one time when the base of the ladder shifted. Hello! I could have decapitated myself if I fell to the ground! That scared me so much. From then on, and still to this day, when I have to do something risky, I say, **"Guardian Angel Alert!"** It makes me feel better knowing that she is at the ready should I need her assistance. My daughter reminds me with: "Mother, you *do* know that you are 72 now!" I have to remind her that I am *only* 72.

When I get home from the gym most weekday mornings, I lift up a Guardian Angel Alert as I head out on my mile prayer walk. It takes me that long to pray for all those sinners on my list including myself. I carry a golf club with me because I'm afraid of loose dogs. I got bit by one when I was little; that fear is still with me.

Many of my Guardian Angel Alerts are lifted upward when I start to clean the house's gutter system. This is a chore that I have to do at least 3-4 times a year. Those 4 huge pecan trees have many branches that hang over the roof. When the trees go through cycles of shedding sticks, caterpillary things, nuts, and leaves, the gutters become full, and they have to be cleaned out. It takes at least 3 hours for me to do the whole system. The long north side of my home is where things get tricky as I can barely fit the ladder in the long flowerbed so I can climb up and reach the gutters. I climb up to the top step and literally hang onto the gutter system with one hand and grab handfuls of clutter with the other. I had a Walter Mitty vision of the ladder starting to fall as I clung to the gutter for dear life. I could see the whole north side of the gutters coming down with me! Thank the Lord for our Guardian Angels!

I want to meet my Guardian Angel when I get to Heaven. I will thank her profusely and tell her how sorry I am that she was assigned to *me*!

The next time you have to do something scary or risky, send up a Guardian Angel Alert of your own. ☺

Angels

Ever since I read Billy Graham's wonderful book, **Angels**, I have been intrigued with them. When Mr. Graham's grandmother was dying, she sat up in bed and said that she saw Jesus with His arms outstretched and Ben, her husband. Wow! That made me think about my husband, Larry. The first person I want to see is Jesus. I love this song entitled, "I Can Only Imagine," by Bart Millard.

> *I can only imagine what my eyes will see*
> *When Your face is before me.*
> *I can only imagine.*

> *Surrounded by Your glory, what will my heart feel?*
> *Will I dance for You, Jesus, or in awe of You be still?*
> *Will I stand in Your Presence, or to my knees will I fall?*
> *Will I sing hallelujah? Will I be able to speak at all?*
> *I can only imagine...*

I believe that after we receive our hug, the greatest hug of all, from Jesus, we will see loved ones. I truly believe that Larry will be there, waiting for me at the pearly gates, maybe with my Guardian Angel. ☺

Hebrews 13:2 says, "Don't forget to be kind to strangers, for some who have done this have entertained angels without realizing it!" A few years ago, I was putting my groceries into my car in the parking lot. Suddenly, this woman appeared like out of nowhere, right beside me. I nearly jumped! She told me that she would help me put up the grocery bags if I could give her some money. I declined her offer to help me with the groceries, but I did give her some money and wished her well. I saw her go to another vehicle and heard her asking for money again. What she said next broke my heart. "I don't know what I ever did to end up like this…" she stated. I watched her as she went to the stoplight, walked across the four-lane highway, and disappeared from my view. I have often thought that I may have met an angel that day.

Coming up my street recently about to finish my prayer walk, I saw a neighbor at the end of his driveway, so I stopped to see how he was doing. He had lost his wife of many years within the last month. Tragically, she died of complications due to needing two surgeries performed close together. Chuck told me this unbelievable story!

A few weeks after losing his wife, he had to go into Fort Worth for a doctor's appointment. When he came out of the building and got into his car, it wouldn't start; he was out of gas. I doubt this had ever happened to him before, but when one is grieving, one doesn't always think straight. I know. He got out of his car, and another car drove up near him. A man and a woman were inside. The man asked if he needed any help. Chuck told him about his problem, and the man said that they would drive him to a gas station to get some gas in a container to bring back for his car. Enroute to the station, out of the blue, the woman said aloud something like this: "Two rods, six inches." Mind you, Chuck had not mentioned his wife's back surgery and what doctors put inside her back, *but* what she said was exactly what had happened during his wife's surgery! He turned around and looked at her, blown away by what she had just said. Chuck got his gas, and this couple drove him back to his car. He got out and after putting down the gas can, he turned to thank them, but they were gone! Like immediately gone…there was no doubt in my neighbor's mind or mine that those two were angels. I still feel this way today.

It's amazing to think about that verse in Hebrews concerning angels. We never know who could be one on any given day.

CHAPTER 12

The Holy Spirit and Jesus Calling

Ephesians 2:10 - "It is God Himself who has made us what we are and given us new lives from Christ Jesus; and long ages ago He planned that we should spend these lives in helping others."

I have to admit that when I was little, I did not understand who the Holy Spirit was. All I knew was the King James Version of the Bible, and it called the Holy Spirit the Holy Ghost. That kind of scared me. When I grew up and studied God's Word, reading about Jesus's gift of the Holy Spirit, it all made sense.

Right after graduating from high school in 1966, I attended Bob Jones University in Greenville, South Carolina, for one semester. Not ready to buckle down and study, I left, got married, and moved to Edmund, Oklahoma. When I returned to college three years later, I took a full load of 18 hours every semester and 10 hours in summer school, and graduated in 2 ½ years. That was so hard, but Larry and I were pretty poor, and I thought that the faster I got my degree, the faster we would be able to go on about our lives and hopefully start a family. In the summer of 1972, I was about to get my degree in elementary education. Graduating in the summer posed an unexpected problem: virtually all of the teaching positions had already been filled by then, and I really needed a job.

One day, in one of my last summer semester's English classes, a professor of mine asked our class if we really believed those stories in the Bible, like the ones about Noah and the ark, Jonah and the whale, etc. He did his best to make us think that they were a bunch of fairy tales. There was dead silence in our classroom. Something welled up inside of me that day; I was SO upset that a professor would put down the Bible in that way! Without even thinking, I spoke up, something I never did in class. I said that I believed *every* word in the Bible to be true. This professor asked me, "So, how do you know they are true?" Instantly I replied: "2nd Peter 1:21: Holy men of God spoke as they were moved by the Holy Spirit." I never ever remembered hearing that Scripture! That was the Holy Spirit speaking through me. My professor did not say a word in reply but moved on with his lesson. When the grades came out, the A I had earned was dropped to a B; he was sending me a message.

Here's the amazing thing about that incident. In our English class was a woman in her 50's or so, going back to college later in life to complete her degree. She heard what I said that day. This sweet lady, who lived 30 miles down the highway in another town, knew the superintendent of her school district. She personally told him what had happened that day. He called me, I interviewed for an opening there, and I was hired to teach 6th grade that fall! God certainly does work in mysterious ways.

In the spring of 2015, big sister, Joyce, and I were talking on the phone about her old car. It was 22 years old with skillions of miles on it, leaking oil like a sieve! The oil had spilled over onto the engine, and it stunk! She drove around in that thing with a *fire extinguisher* beside her on the front seat just in case the oil caught fire and her car burst into flames!!! How would *you* have liked to ride around with her??? Anyhow, I said something about her buying another vehicle. Joyce said that she could not afford to make payments on a new car, much less pay the higher insurance premiums. She said that she needed a car in great shape, not too many miles on it, and an older model, like mine. Then she asked, "Would you sell me yours?" She was kidding, I know, but when we hung up, I heard that "still, small Voice" say to me: "She described *your* car. ***Give her your car!***" I was so surprised and also ashamed to say that I was thinking, "What?" I hadn't had a car payment in over 5 years and did not want another one ever again. My vehicle was a 10-year-old Eddie Bauer Ford Explorer with all the bells and whistles. It only had 47,000 miles on it, garage kept and pristine with one owner, me! I don't ever remember it being in the shop! Well, one should not tell the Holy Spirit no. I give God all the glory. Sis flew out to Texas a few days later and drove "Mr. B," as she called her new ride, back to NC. She was SO happy and appreciative.

In the spring of 2012, my dear neighbor, Sharon, a retired pastor's wife, gave me my first copy of **Jesus Calling**, a wonderful little daily devotional written by Sarah Young. The daily entries in her book are so uplifting and encouraging. I am on my 5th book now. It is so awesome how each day's message is tailor-made for me. My friends say the same thing about theirs.

I have lost track of how many **Jesus Calling** books I have given to others. When I hear that still, small Voice inside me, I know that I need to give one of these books away. I keep two in my car's glove compartment ready to go. By that I mean that I have already filled out the presentation page minus the new recipient's name, of course. On that page I now write, "May you walk and talk with Jesus every day." I also put my favorite bookmark inside. It has the books of the Bible on it, so it's like a table of contents for finding where to look up the wonderful Scriptures included for each day. On the back of these bookmarks I write this Scripture: Isaiah 30:21 – "And if you leave God's paths and go astray, you will hear a Voice behind you say, 'No, this is the way; walk here.'" A little $ is inside, too, should someone need that help. Most importantly, I put a copy of a prayer with the plan of Salvation inside each daily devotional, too. A little letter I wrote about what <u>Jesus Calling</u> has meant to me is included as well.

One day, a few months ago, I took the exit ramp off the highway. There was a stoplight, and it was red. As I sat there waiting for it to turn green, I noticed a man on the grassy median with a sign; he was obviously a person in need. All of a sudden, I thought of the **Jesus Calling** devotional in the glove compartment! The Holy Spirit was speaking to me once again. Time was quickly running out, **and** I was in the wrong lane!!! I grabbed a book and then motioned to the driver on my left that I needed to cross over. He was happy to do so, and when the light turned green, I scooted over into that lane. Having already lowered my window, I handed the man a book. He looked at it, and as I was driving away, he hollered after me: *"This is what I needed!"* Wow! I will always be in awe of the chance to share the Gospel with this man. Or was he really an angel in disguise?

Another Jesus Calling /Holy Spirit moment happened to me a few months ago. I was driving down the highway that runs through our town. As I started crossing the bridge, I saw a man walking along the side of the road. He had a guitar on his shoulder and a knapsack which could have held all of his earthly possessions. Right away, I heard that still, small Voice tell me, "He needs a Jesus Calling." I thought this can't be true! There is no way I could possibly turn around, drive over the bridge again, turn around once more, and hope to find him! All the while, I was driving 45-50 mph in the opposite direction! I kept talking to myself, saying things like this couldn't be right, there was no way for me to accomplish this task, AND I was about to run out of places to pull over and double back in time to find him! Finally, I exited the highway at the very last place I could. I had an overwhelming feeling not to get back onto the highway, doubling back to try to find this man, but to drive parallel to the road through all the parking lots that were close enough to the highway so that I could see him. So, I did. At last I came to the very last parking lot and could drive no further.

All of a sudden, I saw shoes through the brush! It was the man I had seen, AND he left the side of the road and walked into the little parking lot right where I was idling! I was SO shocked! He actually walked right past my car! I finally got my voice back, put down the window, and yelled to the man. He stopped and turned around. I told him I had something for him; he came closer. I wanted to write his name down on the presentation page, so I asked him for it. He looked really surprised and leery, to say the least, answering more in a question tone than statement. "Uh, John?" he replied. I handed him a Jesus Calling, and as he walked away, he said, "Jesus thanks you." Who talks like that? I was so surprised and moved. All the way home I was fighting back tears. I couldn't believe what had just happened to me and this young man. What a phenomenal feeling it is to obey the Holy Spirit's urging! Perhaps, once again, this was another angel...

Col. 4:5 - "Make the most of your chances to tell others the Good News."

CHAPTER 13

Old Age Ain't for the Fainthearted

I was probably in my 30's or 40's when I first heard this saying: "Old Age Ain't for the Fainthearted". I thought it was so funny. It's not so funny now that I am 72, because it is so true.

Older people are my **heroes**. The ailments, surgeries, and other physical maladies they endure are mindboggling to me. Some of my elderly friends have had both knees replaced *plus* one or more hip replacements. Then I hear about lots of cataract surgeries, arthritic pains, osteoporosis problems, heart issues, breathing problems, digestive issues, skin abnormalities, flatulence, balance problems, and the list goes on and on. Our bodies simply begin to wear out as we age.

Then there are the problems concerning memory loss as we grow older. I am thankful that so many of my older friends experience the same memory loss issues as I do! Otherwise, I would surely think that I have dementia or Alzheimer's. My little granddaughter, Princess, asked me why I have so many sticky notes around. If I don't write things down, it has become more than a 50/50 chance that I will forget instead of remember what I need to do, get, etc.

And how about hair loss in women? It seems to be more and

more prevalent these days. I know, as I am in that category. I used to have thick hair, fine, but thick. Then about 6 or 7 years ago, my hair started falling out. I am so close to having to wear a wig. I pray about this condition a lot. I have told myself not to even *think* about having a pity party what with people losing their eyesight or hearing, or our beloved soldiers losing limbs and even their lives. God is in control of our journeys, and if a wig is in my future, so be it. I'll just have to give it a name, like "Winnie," and tell my friends it's okay if they let me know when Winnie's a little crooked. We must keep our senses of humor! ☺

I remember hearing that older people talk a lot about their surgeries, doctor's visits, and funerals. So much of their lives revolve around them! They are my heroes, alright. No, old age ain't for the fainthearted, it's for the stouthearted!

As I close this chapter, I would like to leave you with one of my favorite Bible verses. Deuteronomy 33:25 says: "And may your strength match the length of your days."

CHAPTER 14

You Meet the Nicest People at the Gym

I've been going to our little neighborhood gym for 20 years now. Before that, I lived with out-of-control asthma for 18 years. Finally getting this disease under control enabled me to be able to walk on a treadmill without having an asthma attack. Thank you, Lord, for this gift! I also include lifting weights and doing some sit-ups. Now that I am retired, I can go in the mornings, which is really great.

When I went to the gym after school, I met some super people down there. I still cherish those friendships. Switching to mornings has given me a whole new set of gym buddies. Some have passed away over the years as they were in their 70's and 80's. I hope I'm still going to the gym by then, too!

My 30 minutes on the treadmill are the slowest of my day, *but* they go by much faster when you have friends with whom to visit. The old adage misery likes company is so true. ☺ Plus, we're exercising our jaws and lips.☺

Besides knowing that exercise is good for us, and I think even more so as we age, I go to the gym by 7 A.M. to see my gym buddies. I think the reason why I started going earlier was due to our triple digit summers here in Texas.

It has been fun to get to know these sweet people over the years. We do not meet people by accident. They are meant to cross our paths for a reason. When someone new starts to come, it isn't long before we befriend and get to know them as well. We have lots of laughs, exchange recipes, tell stories, etc. We miss absentees. Hearing about their lives and families is a good thing; I pray for them.

My precious husband passed away suddenly from a heart attack 8 years ago. Lloyd, one of my gym buddies who knew Larry from golfing, called several people that afternoon to tell them. I will never forget the love and support I felt from these wonderful friends. Many of them attended Larry's service.

Many mornings I do not feel like going to the gym to work out, but I know it's good for me, and also, I will need to have a good excuse to report when I go back. Checking off going to the gym each weekday morning is a great feeling.

Happiness is the gym in your rear-view mirror! ☺

I wrote this chapter several weeks ago. Well, yesterday morning I was on my usual treadmill down at the ol' gym. My gym buddy, Ray, was on his favorite one on my left, Barbara was on "her's" on my right, and Ruthie was on her usual one on the right of Barbara. The subject of my book came up, and Barbara asked if I had included a chapter about the gym. I said yes, but that I did not name the names of all my gym buddies for fear I would leave someone out. Almost in unison they said, "I want my name in your book!" Then Barbara said, "And please spell Tennison correctly with an 'i!'" So here I go.

There's Ruthie, Ray, Barbara TENNISON, Bill, Lloyd, John, Pat, Mary, Earl, Ruth Ann, the sisters Charlotte Ann and Linda Sue, Karen, Vic, Annette, Wayne, Dominique, Dave, Fred, Scott, Pam, Doug, Randy, Jackie, Robert, Beth, Steve, Janie, all the sweet, hard-working ladies in Cyndi's exercise class, and I'm sure I have most likely left someone out.

*Our view from the treadmills; we are blessed
indeed. This picture was taken by none other
than: Barbara TENNISON.* ☺

The saga of the gym chapter continues. *This* morning, Mary and Pat were on their favorite treadmills, and I told them what had transpired yesterday. Since they didn't insist upon me including their last names, too, like Barbara TENNISON did, I said, "Well, that's probably a good thing, because if I did, Oprah might want you on her show with me, too." Help me, Rhonda! Pat said, "Then be sure you spell *my* last name correctly! There's no "e" at the end of Featherston!" These people!

I must get this book finished and to a publisher before it becomes a novel! This happened at the gym last week.

I pulled into a parking spot soon after Ruthie had parked; she was waiting for me in the street. As I came around the back of my car, we heard a goose honking very loudly up in the sky somewhere. All of a sudden, he appeared. He was flying very low, like about only 9 feet off the ground, flapping his huge wings and flying straight at us! The honking was deafening! When this big, ol' goose got within 3 feet of us *he dropped his calling card* (or should I say card**s**!)!!! Ruthie and I laughed so hard! I told her that I hoped this was not a bad omen as to how the rest of the day would be. Still guffawing when we walked into the gym, we had to share this funny story with the gym buds, of course. Ruthie told them the goose's *gift* splattered onto my tennis shoes – how rude! ☺

Well, the funniest part of this story is what my son, Nick, said when he called me on his way home from work that afternoon. I told him about the goose and that I thought what happened might have been a bad omen. Nick, ever the optimist, said, "Mother, it was a *good* omen. First of all, he *missed*! **AND**, he was honking to warn you, saying: "Move it, lady! I can't hold it any longer! **Bombs away!!!!!**" I'm still laughing. Whenever I see a goose flying close to the ground, honking for all he's worth, and heading in my direction, I'm running for cover! Cowadunga!

Rachel Anderson

John*

*John, elliptical gym buddy, said recently that he wanted a whole page in my book, so here it is.

132

CHAPTER 15

My Most Embarrassing Moments

My First Jury Duty

I received my first jury duty summons about 25 years ago. This was exciting! At that time, the old courthouse on the town square was where we reported for this important opportunity. I need to interject something here, as I am still baffled by this phenomenon. How on *earth* do people know that when one receives a jury summons 200-300 others have also been summoned AND that all these people are in a jury pool from which 12 will be selected??? Are people born with this knowledge? Did I not get that gene???

Upon entering the building, I saw a woman seated at a table in the hall, so I walked up to her and asked for directions as to where I needed to be. She told me it was upstairs and to go, "right, left, right." I must tell you that I have a major learning disability concerning directionality, so I most likely went left, right, left. Anyhow, miraculously, I ended up in front of this tall, old door that had a sign above it that read: JURY. Wow! I had arrived, literally, for this huge event in my life. I was going to be on a jury! When I entered this room (I am always early), no one was there, but I counted the chairs, and there were 12. I knew that there were 12 people on a jury! Hello! I smelled coffee and saw a box of doughnuts on a table. This was awesome! I helped myself to both and then found a seat and sat down. Soon afterwards, people started arriving. I chatted with them for quite some time when all of a sudden, this man looked at me and asked, "Were you here yesterday?" I replied, "No, I'm reporting for jury duty today." One might have thought I had committed the biggest crime *ever* as he then said, "You can't be in here! This is a formed jury! You have to leave immediately!" So now I knew two things: first, I was in the wrong place, and second, I was now late for my first jury duty. Great. I asked him where I should go, and he said something like down the hall and go left, right, left. I must have gone in the opposite direction again. Another note here – the only thing I knew about a courtroom, having never been inside one, was what I remembered seeing on those old black and white Perry Mason TV shows in the 50's and 60's! So, as I am running down this hall, I *think* I am going to enter the back of the courtroom. All I had to do was slink into the last pew, and no one would know I was late. Oh, no! I came to this door that looked official and ran inside. It was the courtroom, all right, but I ended up standing in front of the jury box just feet away from the judge and the D.A. who was in the middle of giving his voir dire to 300 people!!!!! The door I should have entered was on the opposite side of the room! Everyone was staring at me, and you could have heard a pin drop!!! I was in a state of shock. The D.A. looked at me and asked, "Can I help you?" I was so scared and confused that I started spinning around like a top looking for a place to sit! Finally, I replied that I was reporting for jury duty. Mr. Haddox motioned for me to go that way, straight ahead of him, so I did. Talk about being mortified!!!

The really funny thing about this whole situation is that I saw the D.A. at my elementary school years later where I was teaching. He was coming out of the office, and I told him that he was part of my most embarrassing moment. His wife had just walked up and heard me say that, and she said, "Oh, I have to hear this!" So, I told them, and then I looked at Richard and said, "And then you *picked me for the jury!*" He replied, "Why not?" We had a big laugh. ☺

The Broomstick Skirt and Summer School

I taught summer school many summers. This incident happened in 2000 and was probably the most embarrassing moment of my teaching career. It was awful! Well, after lunch and recess, I read to my kids. They loved it, and I let them sit or lay where they wished. My reading chair was in front of the chalkboard. When I went to it, I noticed that there were 2 chairs there this day, but I didn't think anything of it. Two of my boys were rolling around, playing, so I got on to them, oblivious of what was going on behind me. I went to sit down in my chair and sat down HARD onto the floor instead! There was no chair there (one of the chairs belonged to a student, and she retrieved hers)! In slow motion, I saw my legs go straight up into the air AND my broomstick skirt* slide down around my waist as I exposed my pantyhose to the whole class!!!!! Oh, the kids were roaring with laughter, all right, that is until they heard how hard my head hit the wall! Then there was total silence. I nearly knocked myself out! I sprang up like a gymnast (albeit an old one) and immediately had a terrible headache. I thought I had a concussion, but school must go on! The kids and I had a big laugh because it was pretty funny.

I told my cohearts about this incident after school, and they wondered if the teacher next door to me heard my head hit the wall. We found Jean, and I asked her if she remembered hearing a loud bang on her wall about 12:10, to which she replied, "Why, yes, I did. Yoanzet remarked, 'Mrs. Adkins, I think they're wrestling in Mrs. Anderson's room!'" Ha!

When school took up that August and I told my teaching partner about making a spectacle of myself in summer school, Patsy asked me what in the world was I doing wearing pantyhose during the inferno (temps from 107-113 degrees!). I told her, "Let's not even go there!!!"

*For those of you who do not know what a broomstick skirt is, it is simply a skirt with an elastic waist made with many yards of fabric. I ordered this skirt from a mail order catalog because I loved the pretty fabric. It arrived in a tube! I couldn't believe someone would pack a skirt this way because it had a million wrinkles in it! Little did I know that a broomstick skirt was **supposed** to look wrinkled! I thought, I'll just have to iron those wrinkles out! I ironed and ironed and ironed!!!!! The next day was Sunday, so I decided to wear my pretty new skirt to church. When the congregation went to sit down after singing a hymn, I think my skirt flared out and covered up two people on either side of me, there was SO much fabric! My friend told me after church to put the skirt back into the tube for a while to restore the wrinkles!

I Pulled my Pants Down at the Gym

This incident happened at our little neighborhood gym several years ago. It was a Saturday morning in January, and I was about to leave for the gym. I always wore shorts even on really cold days like this one was. My husband told me to put some wind pants on over my shorts because it was so cold outside. Since I was having my first stress test soon, I decided I would because I might be wearing them over shorts for my test, and I would know if I'd get too hot wearing that extra layer.

My torture of choice is the treadmill. There were lots of people there that morning (of course!). The treadmills are across the front with lots of ellipticals and bicycles behind them. After only a few minutes into my 30-minute walk, I got hot and decided that the wind pants had to go. I put the machine on pause, stepped to the side, and pulled down my wind pants. Having forgotten to unzip the leg bottoms, I was really struggling to get them off over my tennis shoes. All of a sudden, or so it seemed, I felt a draft on my legs. Oh, I hadn't *just* pulled down my wind pants; ***I pulled down my shorts, too!!!*** I think I set a Guinness Book of World Records' time for how fast I pulled up those britches!!! I couldn't believe that I didn't hear anyone laugh, or clear their throats and say, "Ahem! Lady, Lady! Tsk! Tsk! Tsk!" I was SO embarrassed! I didn't dare turn around, so I stayed on the treadmill until everyone left the room!!! Talk about exhausted! To this day, I have no idea who saw me expose my underwear to everyone! Maybe that's a *good* thing!

What Happens at La Quinta *Stays* at La Quinta (or *should!*)

My husband, Larry, always stayed in La Quinta hotels when he was a travelling salesman. He and I and our daughter, Buddy, stayed overnight in one on our way home from visiting son, Nick, and his family in North Carolina one Christmas break. In the morning, we went to the dining area to enjoy a delicious continental breakfast before we headed back to Texas. There was a good crowd there, also (wouldn't you know it???). After our meal, as Larry and I were walking across the room, Larry looked at me and ***announced***, "I heard that!" At that precise moment, he plummeted from the True Husband Pedestal he had been on all of our marriage. Had he only said, "Excuse me!" and taken the blame, he would have still been there. When we got to the elevator and the door opened, I walked straight to a corner, like a little one who was in big trouble. ☹ Just then Buddy walked in, and *she* proclaimed, "I heard that all the way over at the juice display counter, Mother!" I told this highly embarrassing moment to my BFF, Marsh, but she couldn't figure out what happened, so I had to tell her that I t_ _ted!!!!! The missing letters are the same vowels! I mean really, even the Queen of England...

Thank the Lord I never had to see any of those people ever again! Just so you know, it took Larry a short time to be back on the coveted True Husband Pedestal once again. ☺

Peggy and "The Whiners"

Peggy was a wonderful kindergarten teacher at Acton Elementary here in town. I was teaching 4th grade at that time. She and I loved "The Whiner" family on Saturday Night Live back in the 80's. The parents, kids, all of their family members would whine. Peggy and I only did this after school when we would run into each other in the hall, the workroom, etc. Peggy might say, in her best Whiner voice: "Raaaaccchhell, how *arreee* youuuu?" I'd reply in *my* best Whiner voice: "Oooohhh, Peggggggyyyy, I'm goooddd, and youuuuuuuu?" We would get so tickled.

Well! I had to go to the grocery store after school one day. There were 3-4 people behind me in line when I got to the checker. As the checker was ringing up my purchases, all of a sudden, I heard, in a rather *loud,* familiar voice say, "Raaaaccchhell, iisss thaaaaatt you, Raaaaccchhelll?" I couldn't believe my ears! We were out in *public*, for goodness sake!!! Well, I could not, with a clear conscience, hang my sweet teacher friend out to dry, so of course I had to reply: "Peeggggyyyy! Diddd youuuu haavvvee aaa gooddd daaaaaaayyyyy?" And so on and so forth! Oh, help me, Lord! I can't remember how other people reacted that day, it was like an out-of-body experience, but I can tell you that Peggy and I had a big laugh in school the next day. ☺

I Thessalonians 5:16 - "Always be joyful."

CHAPTER 16

Wrong Words to Songs

W e've all probably done this, or at least heard someone else do this: sing the wrong words to a song. Ma enjoyed a cup of tea most afternoons. One day, when my big sister, Joyce, a second grader, came home from school, she was singing "My Country 'tis of Thee." Ma asked her to sing it again for her, so little Joycie sang, "My country 'tis of thee, Sweet land of Lipton tea, of thee I sing…" Too cute!

Joyce would take us younger siblings for a ride in her cool '58 Chevy sedan. She proceeded to sing along with the song playing on the radio, only *she* was singing: Brotherly *love*, **Brotherly** love…" I think us kids all said in unison, "It's *not* 'Brotherly love, it's **Mother-in-law**!!!" Sheesh!

I've always loved this song by Dewey Bunnell beginning with these words: "I rode through the desert on a horse with no mane, it felt good to be out in the rain…" but I always felt so badly for the horse that had no mane. Then someone corrected me saying, "It's not a horse with no *mane*! It's a horse with no *name!!!*" To add insult to injury, my son recently told me that it also wasn't out *in* the rain but *of* the rain. He said, "Mother, he's in the desert where it doesn't rain. He's been in the rain. It's out *of* the rain!" Give me a break!

One year when teaching 4th grade, I noticed that my little Ashley wasn't present, I asked the class if they had seen her. Some of the kids told me that she went to the office because she was going to be the one that morning to sing, "The National Anthem" on the intercom for the whole school. Ashley never told me this; I was so proud of her courage!

Well! When our principal, Heather, came on the intercom with the daily announcements, she then announced that Ashley from Mrs. Anderson's 4th grade class was going to sing "The Star-spangled Banner." So, we all stood up and faced the flag with hands over our hearts, listening to that precious little Ashley's voice. She was doing great, aside from mumbling through the words she didn't know: "O say can you see, by the dawn's early light, what so proudly we hailed, (mumble, mumble) …last gleaming……. (more mumbles) …were so gallantly streaming…. THEN she sang in her big voice, "AND THE ROBIN'S RED BREAST," (the kids looked at me!! We couldn't help giggling; I pretended all was good!) "the bombs bursting in air" . . . more mumbles, but all I kept hearing was the robin's red breast! "Oh, say, does that star-spangled ba-ann-annnner yet waaaaavvvveeee (mumble, mumble), and the home…of the….braaaavvvveeee!" ☺

I knew that I only had a few minutes before Ashley came into the room, so I told the kids how proud I was of her, that they should be, too, and when she entered, we were going to give that little girl a standing ovation and brag and brag on her, and we did! Heather (not just my principal, but also my friend) saw me later and asked me, "Why didn't you tell me Ashley didn't know the words to the anthem?" Hello! I told her that I didn't even know she was doing this, AND why didn't *she* have her audition??? There were lots of smiles exchanged that day between teachers and staff. Kids are so dear.

Parents can be a great source of embarrassment to their teenagers, as we all know (and vice versa, I may add!). I swear, when Buddy was in junior high (okay, I'm really dating myself here – middle school), if she could have convinced her friends that she had been hatched from an egg and didn't even have a human mother, she would have.

So, she and I were riding somewhere in the car, and I started to sing along to a popular Hall & Oates song playing on the radio: "Your kiss is on my lips, your kiss is on my lips..." Correction: "Mother! It's 'Your kiss is on my *list*, not my *lips*! Oh, give me a break! I told her that it made a whole lot more sense to have a kiss on the *lips*, not on some *list*! The rolling of the eyes, for sure.

Then another time I knew that this knowledge would really impress Buddy. We were at our local photographer's studio to have her senior pictures taken. Music was playing on the intercom, and I commented to the photographer and her that I knew this group (having only seen their name in writing). "Oh, that's the Inks!" The look on Buddy's face was sheer horror. What? When we got to the car afterwards, she said: "Mother! That was SO embarrassing! The group singing is *not* the *Inks*. They're INXS!" Pronounced "In Excess". I mean really!

When I was little, and perhaps some of you reading this did the same, I thought that the hymn, "Bringing in the Sheaves" was "Bringing in the *Sheep*." My friend, Ruthie, and I grew up with clotheslines to hang up all the laundry to dry as clothes dryers hadn't been invented yet. Well! Ruthie was singing, "Bringing in the *Sheets!*" ☺

One Sunday afternoon, Nick and I and the grandkids were playing Phase 10, a really fun card game. I had a CD playing some golden oldies. When Elvis's, "You Ain't Nothin' But a Hound Dog" came on, I started singing along: "You ain't nothin' but a hound dog, crockin' all the time..." Well! Cam said, "Gramma! What did you say?" So, I sang those lyrics again, and he told me that it was *not* "crockin'" but "cryin'!" What??? Of course, Nick and Princess agreed with Cam. I decided to poll people to see what they were singing. I caught neighbor, Bill, out in his yard and asked him, "What did Elvis sing in "You ain't nothin' but a hound dog, (humming) all the time?" He commenced to sing, "You ain't nothin' but a hound dog, *barking* all the time." What a HOOT! Then I polled a gym buddy, Ammie, and she sang, "You ain't nothin' but a hound dog, *running* all the time." HA! I listened very closely to Elvis singing that song, and I swear he is saying, "crockin'!" Have fun with this – poll family members and friends, and see what they are saying. Surely, someone else sings, "crockin'", too.

I firmly believe that God has a wonderful sense of humor, and when he hears little ones singing the wrong words to songs in church, He is smiling, too.

Psalm 66: 1 & 2: "Sing to the Lord, all the earth! Sing of His glorious name! Tell the world how wonderful He is!"

CHAPTER 17

The Neighbors and Banana Nut Bread

I honestly cannot remember how this tradition began or how long we have been doing this. First of all, I must tell you that I have some of the best neighbors on the planet. I told my husband once that if we ever won the lottery, I would never sell our home and move away because we could never replace these dear people. They would do anything for me and vice versa.

I have been baking banana nut bread for many years, and over those years I have tried a number of different recipes. I would make tweaks, keeping the ingredients I liked, changing others, and adjusting amounts, etc. Finally, I have come up with this recipe and kept it for years. Well, actually, I think I made a couple more tweaks to it like last year or so. Having 4 large pecan trees enables me to add lots of delicious pecans.

Well, I'm sure that one day I gave two of my across-the-street neighbors each a mini loaf of banana nut bread. They loved it! Yeah! I started making 4 mini loaves instead of one big loaf because I can get them to bake more evenly, *and* they are perfect for sharing. I sliced the little loaves for the neighbors and myself. Since I kept 2 loaves, and each loaf ended up with 8-9 slices, I could make my

2 loaves last nearly 3 weeks. I didn't realize until recently that my neighbors' mini loaves lasted like 2 *days*! Ha! When my son, Nick, moved into our development, I included him in our rotation as he loves banana nut bread, too. The neighbors are glad because now I bake these more often as my one loaf doesn't last as long as two did! ☺

I baked some banana nut bread on Monday. When the loaves have cooled a little, I put them into sandwich baggies and text the neighbors, the Waddills and the Lebsacks, with this message: "Warm banana nut bread, anyone? Anyone???" If they are home, they come running, well, walking kinda quickly as they are getting elderly now. Sharon came and got her's and Lee's, but I didn't hear back from Bill and Diann. So, I texted Bill yesterday: "Cold banana nut bread, anyone? Anyone???" If he hadn't come over, my next text was going to be: "Frozen banana nut bread, anyone? Anyone???" I must say here that I am paid back in kind with delicious food from them. I am SO blessed! Thank you, Jesus.

Banana Nut Bread

1 stick of (real) butter, softened
¾ C. sugar (or a little bit more)
1 t. soda
1 t. salt
1 t. (real) vanilla
2 (real) large eggs
3 ripe bananas (I use medium ones), mashed
1 2/3 C. flour (probably a little bit more)
1/3 - ½ C. (real) sour cream
¾ - 1 C. chopped pecans

Preheat oven to 350 degrees (340 for dark pans). Grease and flour 4 mini loaf pans, 1 reg., or a 1 doz. cupcake pan.

Cream butter & sugar in mixing bowl until light & fluffy. Add eggs; beat. Add bananas; mix. Add vanilla; mix. Fold in sour cream. Add dry ingredients; mix well. Stir in nuts.

Pour into prepared pans. Bake 32-35 minutes for mini loaves. Test for doneness. Turn out onto wire rack to cool. Slice. Store in Ziploc sandwich baggies. These freeze well. YUM! YUM!

CHAPTER 18

Sammy!!!

I call all squirrels "Sammy." We are arch enemies and have been for 32 years now. I used to think that squirrels were so cute. Not! They are very destructive animals.

All of the homes on my street were built in an old pecan orchard, so we have lots and lots of pecan trees. I have 4 huge ones, and all of the neighbors have pecan trees as well. I see Sammy and his friends virtually every day. They love to eat pecans, so it's like Restaurant Row here! It is WAR on Bueno Drive. Who do you think is winning?

He loves to chew into patio furniture pads, ripping out the soft padding to use in his nests. Lovely. Sammy also chews into the wooden siding trying to get into our attics. It is a good thing that he hasn't been successful in doing so at my house (I have hired carpenters over the years to replace the damage he's done in trying), but he has gotten into some of my neighbors' attics, chewed through wiring, causing all kinds of damage and problems. Sammy got into my neighbors' car by getting under the hood. He then chewed up the wiring to the tune of @ $1,000 worth of damage. When they got their car back, I'll be if Sammy didn't do that again!!! He chewed around the holes in my TWO birdhouses to make the entrances bigger so that HE could reside in them. Hello? It isn't called a squirrel house!!!

One year, Sammy made a hole in the screen on our chimney top. He would climb inside, stick his little face out, and I swear he would smirk at us!!! Man! I would then try to pelt him with pecans (his favorite food!) to make him get out, like that was going to work. The inevitable happened a few days later; Sammy fell 16 feet down the chimney, landing on top of the flue in our fireplace. Thank the Lord it was closed!!! He was jumping and scratching for all he was worth, trying to get out. Great, just great. After calling our pest control man, the VFD, Animal Control, Security, etc., none of which could help us, we came up with a few plans of our own. All of them were far too risky as Sammy was now a horribly sooty black ball of adrenalin who would surely escape if we opened the flue, wreaking havoc all over our home. Sammy expired in a few days (we felt badly), so my husband and I decided to open the flue and remove him before he started to smell. The plan was that I would hold a box, and Larry would very slowly open the flue. Well, we thought that the black, sooty tail *moved*! We both yelled and jumped a foot into the air!!! Good **thing** we didn't try to get him out alive! What a mess that would have been!

Several years ago, I told Larry that all I wanted for Mother's Day was a slingshot. I thought that I would shoot pecans (my ammo) at Sammy when he came into our yard, and that would scare him away. I'm so sure! I'm sending him his favorite food each time! He might think we're friends! I keep my slingshot and ammo on a little table right outside of the patio door. One time he and I were like 4 feet apart. Sammy was in the V of a pecan tree, and we locked eyes for several seconds. I thought that he was going to leap onto my NECK!

In December of 2012, about a week after my beloved husband, Larry, passed away, I read this Bible verse: Psalms 94:19 – "Lord, when doubts fill my mind, when my heart is in turmoil, quiet me, and give me renewed hope and cheer." I didn't have a problem with the hope, but there was no cheer in our home, and I didn't know when there would be.

One morning, Buddy, my precious daughter who stayed with

me for about 10 days after her dad's funeral, was in the living room drinking her coffee when I stopped to talk to her. I was facing the backyard, and all of a sudden, I saw Sammy in a pecan tree. In mid-sentence, I growled, "SAMMY!" and took off for the patio, my slingshot, and ammo. I started peppering Sammy with pecans but didn't come close to hitting him, as usual. Well! He was in the "V" of the tree again, and he turned his backside to me. How rude!!! I took aim and hit him dead center! Suddenly, he plummeted to the ground! I turned and looked at the windows to see if Buddy was still watching, hoping that she wasn't. Oh, yes, she was, and when we looked at each other, we had the same exact expression on our faces: eyes and mouths wide open in sheer disbelief! I looked back at Sammy. He got up slowly and was hobbling across the backyard. Buddy and I had a big laugh – that was our cheer! ☺ The Lord knew we needed some that day.

Over the 32 years that I have lived in my home, I think that I have grazed Sammy's tail with a pecan like half a dozen times. When my dear former next-door neighbor, Jean, would be sitting on her patio, and she'd hear my ammo hit the fence, I'd hear her say under her breath, "Dead Eye." Too funny! I miss her.

CHAPTER 19

Your Word is Your Bond

(or The Cannonball Controversy)

Have you ever felt like your kids and/or grandkids were conspiring against you? Well, let me tell you about the cannonball controversy.

My son and grandkids sometimes come over for lunch on Sundays after church. One time, Cam said, "Gramma, you told us a year *or two* ago that you would do a cannonball off the diving board at the club pool, and you never have." Hello! This was news to me! I looked at my son for some support here, but he was nodding his head affirmatively.

After my family left, I called my daughter in Chicago and told her what happened, explaining to her that surely I did not say that. *She* responded with, "Oh, yes, you did, Mother! I was there when you said that!" I just could not believe my ears. Then I thought, these people know that Gramma doesn't have the memory she used to have, and they are conspiring against me to see me make a fool of myself!

The next time Nick, Cam, and Princess came for Sunday lunch, Cam asked me again when I was going to do my cannonball. I asked him why he wanted to know, and he said, "I want to call my friends so we can stand on the side of the pool and say, "Gram-maw! Gram-maw! Gram-maw!" Oh, help me, Lord!

Over the years, I have worked on practicing what one preaches and that your word is your bond. I simply had no choice here; I had to do this cannonball. I wasn't about to lose face with my kids and grandkids.

So, the first thing I did was look in my bottom dresser drawer to find my bathing suit which I hadn't worn in years. It was my favorite, black with little white polka dots. When I held it up to look at it, I could nearly see right through the fabric in several spots! It had disintegrated over the 20+ years I'd had it! Thank the Lord I noticed this! I don't even want to think about what could have happened to my vintage bathing suit had I worn it at the pool. I only had one more, a suit with a bright Hawaiian print. It would have to do.

I called Nick and told him for the three of them to meet Gramma at the pool at 10:55 the next Friday. Adult lap swimming and water aerobics were from 11:00 to 11:30, so there would hardly be any one there. Phew! I'm thinking most Grammas' bods look like mine, which is not a pretty sight. Doing this cannonball for my family was an act of pure love, let me tell you, and honor as well. How on earth do I get myself into these situations???

The weeks before I did this, I had worked myself up into a frenzy. First of all, I am afraid of water over my head. My husband, Larry, was a great swimmer, diver (on his college fraternity's team), and lifeguard. Buddy and Nick were both excellent swimmers, and they also lifeguarded several summers. To compound my fear of deep water is the fact that I am an asthmatic, so I was afraid that I would not be able to hold my breath long enough. I mean I could faint underwater or have the big one!!! My BFF, Marsh, I guess thinking that she was funny, downloaded several people going off diving boards and biting it! Some were quite elderly (all guys, us gals know better!), and I think they must have hurt more than their pride from the looks of those videos. I was in quite a state, but a couple of days before the main event, I lifted up a prayer and gave this challenge to the Lord. I immediately felt better; it was going to be okay.

I got to the pool a few minutes before Nick and the kids. I know that Nick told Cam and Princess that Gramma was scared to do the cannonball. When they got there, they ran up to me and gave me hugs. Talk about making me feel better! I did my cannonball, albeit the ugliest one in its history with the smallest splash *ever*, but that's okay. I got it done! Yeah!

In the future, I hope I will be very careful what I say. Good thing I didn't say that I would bungee jump into the Grand Canyon!!! I want to leave you with this verse from Proverbs, one of my favorite books in the Bible: Proverbs 10:19: "Don't talk so much. You keep putting your foot in your mouth. Be sensible, and turn off the flow!"

CHAPTER 20

How to Have a True Husband and How to Be a True Husband

The joint title of this chapter is self-explanatory as you can't have a true husband without your husband being one. Husbands will love this: to have one, you have to spoil him...a lot. Of course, a true husband deserves this. Let me explain...

I won the lottery when I met and married Larry. He was the epitome of what a true husband should be: loving, kind, honest, devoted, funny, thoughtful, sincere, caring, considerate, hard-working, conscientious, appreciative, and many more. He was easy to spoil.

Over the 44 years we had together as husband and wife, I tried to take very good care of him. When we were first married, Larry just wore skivvies to bed with no t-shirt. He would get cold! Hello! So, I had to domesticate him. I bought him some knee-length pajama bottoms and short-sleeved tees for the warm months, long-sleeved tees and long bottoms for the cool months, then flannel bottoms for winter.

One Christmas break, Buddy was home for the holidays. She

and I were about to leave early for the gym since her dad was still sleeping. Before we left, I did what I did every morning: warmed up a piece of my homemade banana nut bread that he loved, and put it on a little paper plate on the end table in the living room next to the loveseat where he sat to read his paper. Having already made the coffee, I put it in the carafe with his coffee cup next to the bread on the table. I had gone outside to retrieve the paper so that it would be dry and warm for him, also. I turned on the little electric stove with its pretty "flame" for ambiance. Just as we were about to leave, Larry emerged from the bedroom wearing his Brooks' Brothers blue plaid flannel robe over his Land's End pajamas and his L.L. Bean's Wicked Good slippers. That's when Buddy exclaimed: "Mother! You spoil him *way* too much!" Perhaps I did, but it was worth it because he had become a true husband.

When Larry retired, he would golf 4-5 days a week. This was fine with me because I got so much more done with him not under foot and at home every day. A couple of times a month, or there about, he and his fishing buddies would go on 3-day trips and have so much fun. That's when I could make a big mess piecing my quilts, with the ironing board up in the kitchen and the sewing machine on the dining room table, etc. Virtually every fishing trip, I would send a delicious homemade meal with him for the guys to enjoy. Sometimes, I'd send a breakfast casserole, too, and perhaps a dessert. Larry was always so appreciative of these goodies.

I'm not telling you all this to pat myself on the back. The moral to this chapter, if you will, is that if you spoil your hubby, you will have a true husband, and he will be one. Because I spoiled him, he spoiled me. Larry's burgers, steaks, blackened fish that he caught, and smoked meats were to die for, and I miss his grilling so much. Over the years, he always took my vehicles to the car wash for me and also had the oil changed. He took care of the yard; I tended to the flowerbeds. Laughter was important in our home, and hardly a day went by that he didn't make me laugh. We both worked to provide for our family and retired within a year of each other.

Larry loved me, and he knew that I loved him. We were a team. True love is caring more about your spouse's happiness than your own. So, to summarize what I've been trying to say is this: the way we treat our mates and vice versa has so much to do with a happy marriage. It definitely works both ways.

I'm sharing a story with you here because I think it is important. Five months before we moved into our new home in Granbury in 1988, Larry caught a 9 lb. largemouth bass on Lake Okeechobee in Florida. He took it to a taxidermist to have it mounted with a plaque stating these details: caught by Larry Anderson, 9 lbs., 01/17/88, Lake Okeechobee. When we finally moved into our new home and were unpacking, setting up everything, Larry hung his big fish above the mantel in the living room for all to see; he was so proud of his fish, as he should have been. Well, a few months later, when I had finished decorating our home office with lots of fishing memorabilia, I thought, Dad's fish would look great in here! Having never seen another fish hung in one's living room, I thought the office would be a better place for "Walter, Jr.," as we called him (remember "On Golden Pond?"). I honestly did not think that Larry would even notice. When he came home from golfing, his missing fish was the *first* thing he noticed! To this day, I will never forget what he said to me: "Mother, all these years that we've been married, you enjoyed decorating our homes, and I never said a thing about anything you chose to do. Then the one time I wanted to do something, hanging my fish in the living room, you moved it." That broke my heart! I ran to the office, got Walter, Jr., and hung him back up in his place of honor where he has remained the 32 years I've lived here. Walter, Jr., still proudly hangs in the living room even though Larry has been gone 7 years now. I decorate Larry's big catch anew each season.

I used to think that the best thing I did was taking really good care of my husband. Oh, I miss that immensely! What I would give to spoil that "true husband" some more, but God had other plans. I cherish the years we had together and the memories we made. Spoil each other because you never know when that time will end. I can honestly say that I have no regrets concerning the way I took care of Larry. Remember when his sweet mother told me that he was spoiled but that "he didn't take to it?" Ha! So, I took up where she left off, **and** he is getting spoiled in heaven by her some more! ☺

CHAPTER 21

Teach Your Mate Before It's Too Late

The title of this chapter speaks volumes. I imagine that the majority of us don't, or didn't, do this. It never entered my mind to teach Larry the things I knew how to do in and around our home, nor did I think to ask him to do the same.

My husband took care of mowing, weed eating, edging, fertilizing, etc. the lawn and all the upkeep concerning that equipment. When Larry passed away so unexpectedly, of course there was no time to ask him questions then. I didn't even know how to start the lawn mower or the other battery powered and gas-powered tools. The yard was just too much for me, especially during our triple digit Texas summers. So, I hired Antonio, a highly-respected lawn service owner, and his crew. They do an outstanding job for a nominal fee. I don't know what I would do without their help.

I live in a community that has an 18-hole golf course and a Par 3 course as well. Many people have their own golf carts, and they can drive them everywhere here. Larry loved his golf cart; he golfed 4-5 days a week with it. Several months after his dad passed away, my son, Nick, went golfing with his Dad's cart. I don't know how many holes he got to play before the golf cart died. A friend towed it back to my house for Nick. All I knew about the cart, besides that it ran on batteries and not gas, was remembering Larry charging the batteries up using the cart's battery charger. We tried hooking the cart up to the charger, but it still wouldn't work. The cart got picked up by a repairman, and the diagnosis was very bad: all 6 batteries had been fried because there was not a drop of water in them. I had no clue that the batteries needed to have a certain amount of water kept in them so that this wouldn't happen. It cost me over $900 to replace them. Had I learned how to maintain the golf cart before I lost Larry, this never would have happened. Talk about a costly lesson.

In our marriage, Larry took care of the stocks and bonds, 401k, etc., and I handled the checking/savings accounts. I had no clue what he did concerning our "portfolio" (and still don't). Once in a while, we would meet with our stock broker. When Scott and Larry were conversing about these things, it went right over my head and out the window! Thank God my son, Nick, is very knowledgeable about this subject. Scott speaks to Nick now so that I don't have to be concerned.

I mentioned earlier that Larry took care of our vehicles. I didn't know that the sticker inside the driver's door let one know when to get the oil changed, or that the sticker on the front windshield had a date not to go past concerning getting our vehicles inspected, or that the golf cart had a sticker on it that lasted a year before one would get a ticket here for a past due golf cart sticker!!!

It's still difficult for me to talk about what happened concerning changing the water filter in our fridge a month after losing my beloved husband. The prompt on the fridge said that it was time to change the water filter. I knew that I had the owner's manual (Nick says that I have every one known to man! Kids!), so I read up on how to do this and to find out about the correct filter to buy. The next day, I was ready. How hard could it be? Well! I must have turned the old filter too far to the right (left?) because Niagara Falls happened in the fridge!!!!! I'm not kidding you; it was like someone had turned on a faucet full blast. The fridge was inundated with the deluge within seconds. I had no idea what to do except pray. Within seconds, I noticed a pitcher drying in the sink, so I ran to get it, ran back, and put it under the gushing water. Then I grabbed another pitcher in a cupboard. When one was nearly full, I took it and replaced that one with the empty one. This all happened quite rapidly. I was beside myself trying not to really start crying. It had to be the Holy Spirit telling me to call security for help, so I did, all the while changing those pitchers out very quickly! The nicest guard came, saw the situation, went out into the garage and found the gadget one uses to turn off the water outside. Then he came back in and put the new filter on, turned on the water outside, and everything was good again. I had quite a lake in the kitchen to clean up, but thank the Lord for sending Skip who knew exactly what to do to help me. I did cry when he left, I was so shaken by that horrible experience. To this day, I cannot change the filter; I am still too frightened.

I should have taught Larry my jobs: how to balance our checkbook and how I pay the bills (including where everything needed to do so is located), how to operate the washer, dryer, and dishwasher. Then there's how to do the laundry, take care of the flowerbeds, etc. I think Larry's flowers would be artificial ones. I can only imagine his arrangements.☺

Please, dear readers, teach your mate before it's too late. Don't forget to tell each other where important information is located, also. Luckily, Larry and I used one filing system, and our files are in alphabetical order. Nick helped me to find tax information, where the titles to his dad's vehicle and boat were, and what I needed to do to sell them. He also made a long list of all the things I needed to do, like contact Social Security, order several death certificates, etc. When one has been blindsided by grief, one can barely get out of bed, never mind think about the myriad of items that must get done. Both kids, Buddy and Nick, helped me so much, and I know that my Heavenly Father was, and is, with me each step of the way on my journey to Heaven.

CHAPTER 22

I Saved the Best for Last

The worst day of my life became the best.

Larry and I married on August 3rd, 1968; he was 23, and I was 20. We had 44 wonderful years together. In one of his Valentine's Day cards that I saved, he wrote: "Please be my Valentine because I am a little bit spoiled, and I love you!" A little bit? I miss that man so much. . .

Larry was a big napper, and he would take a nap every day that he could. Commercial throws were never long or wide enough for his comfort. One year I had an epiphany. I am a hand quilter and love to piece and quilt homemade quilts, so I thought, why don't you make Daddy (what I usually called him) his very own custom nap quilt? I can't believe that I didn't think to do this years earlier.

When he came in from a hard day of golfing one time and was going to take his nap, I had him lie down on the bed so that I could "measure" him. I measured his length and width, adding extra inches so that the nap quilt (per his instructions) would be long enough for him to tuck under his feet to keep them warm in cold weather, and wide enough so that when he turned over, his backside would not be exposed to any drafts. ☺ I made his custom nap quilt with fabric I had, one of which had a fishing motif. Perfect! Larry absolutely loved his nap quilt. I can still hear the dresser drawer pulls as he would retrieve his favorite quilt.

Two weeks before he passed away, one morning, out of the blue, Larry said to me, "You give the greatest hugs." That statement still brings me comfort to this day. All that time I thought he was just "assuming the position" to please me. When we would go to sleep, Larry would roll over onto his right side with his knees bent. I would scoot up close to him with my knees bent right under his. Then I would snake my left arm under his left arm, reach across his tummy, and hold onto his right arm. I'd kiss his neck and back, and we'd say to each other, "Night-night, love you, see you in the morning," which is what we said to our children all those years of raising them.

After I lost Larry so suddenly and unexpectedly, and it took me several months before I could write "Larry's Story." I've added more details for this book. I wanted people to know what happened because Larry couldn't tell them.

Larry's Story

Larry was raised in the Church of Christ by a Christian mother. He never made the commitment to be saved, for whatever reason. I know that MaMa was saved. I held her hand the last 24 hours of her life in M.D. Anderson Cancer Hospital in Houston, Texas, January 14-15, 1983. I saw the expression on her face when she passed away, one of peace and joy. She was 68 years old. Larry and I couldn't understand why MaMa had to suffer with bone cancer for months before she died, or why God took her from us. He chooses to reveal some mysteries to us, and some He does not. We have to trust Him.

I was saved when I was 9 years old. To be saved when one is young is so awesome. I cannot say that I always acted as a Christian should have. There were 2 times in my life, two 10-year periods, when no one would have known that I was a Christian, sad to say. It was during the first time that I met and married Larry.

I would go to church on and off during the 44 years we were

married. When our kids, Buddy and Nick, were little, I took them to Sunday school and "big church" so they would learn about God and Jesus and be saved, too, and praise the Lord, they both are. I could never talk Larry into going to church with us.

Over the years, I would try to witness to Larry about his salvation. So, did Buddy. After Larry passed away, I found a letter that Buddy had written to her dad when she was a teenager about accepting the Lord as his Savior. I had also given him an important article concerning his salvation; he kept both of these in his top dresser drawer for over 20 years. Periodically, I would ask Larry if he would sit down with me so that we could talk about his salvation; he never would do this. I prayed for this precious man for over 40 years.

A couple of weeks before Larry passed away, I asked him one evening if he would ever sit down with me and talk about this most important commitment concerning his salvation. He replied, "Probably not." I was so stunned. I felt like bawling but held it in. I remember thinking of all the years I had been praying for him, and I thought, "I am not praying for him anymore!" Hello! That was Satan getting to me. Then I thought, I will just have to pray for him twice as much! The Bible tells us to pray without ceasing. I knew that Larry did not want his life to change one iota; he loved his life so much. On Sunday mornings when I would leave for church, he headed to a local restaurant to have breakfast with his cronies. Then they would play in their Sunday golf game. Larry golfed 4-5 days a week and went on fishing trips every other week or so with his beloved fishing buddies. Larry did not want his wonderful life to change one bit. Matthew 10:39 says: "If you cling to your life, you will lose it; but if you give it up for Me, you will save it." Little did he know that when one accepts Christ as one's Savior, one wants to make changes.

The day I lost Larry was as normal a morning as could be. We had breakfast together; we never got to have lunch because we were in our local hospital's ER. At first, I was told that Larry didn't have a heart attack. Thank you, Lord! Sweet neighbors, the Waddills, came up to check on Larry and me. I told them that it looked like Larry was going to be okay; perhaps he just pulled some muscles when he carried those heavy boxes of pecans earlier. I called Nick, as he was about to leave his job 40 minutes away and come to the hospital, and told him not to, that Dad didn't have a heart attack after all. Then I was told that he had a *little* heart attack. It seemed like forever that I had to stay out in the hall. The door to Larry's room was closed. I stood there all alone for a long time, then one of Larry's fishing & golfing buddies, Corky, felt led to come up to the hospital to check on us. God knew I needed him to be there with me. A hospital liaison woman stood beside us for a while. I finally asked her if she would please go into Larry's room to see what was happening. When she opened his door, they were performing CPR on him!!! I had no idea that things were going south so fast! After a while, a nurse came out and told me to get to Parkland Hospital in Dallas as quickly as possible; Larry was in critical condition; the helicopter crew was there. When she went back inside Larry's room and closed the door, something told me not to leave right then. Corky and I waited and waited. Finally, the door opened, and everyone, including the helicopter crew, came out; it looked like all of them had been crying. That is when I knew Larry didn't make it. I remember saying, "No! No! No!" many times, then telling Corky, "I was supposed to get him saved first!"

I am having a very difficult time writing this without totally losing it...even after 7 years, the pain and grief are still there...

I hurried into Larry's room and just fell onto him. I had to close those beautiful, blue eyes; there were tears in his, too. Thank God that Corky was there as he started calling my son and others with Larry's phone. I sat down in a chair beside Larry's gurney and laid my head on his chest. I just could not leave him. Nick came; I could tell that he had been crying. He adored his father. He pulled up another chair, and we both stayed there for a long time. The ER staff was sweet to let us do that. I knew when we left him, that was it. We would never see him again, or so I thought.

I remember telling God all those years of praying for Larry's salvation that the one thing I could not bear to have happen to me was for me to die or Larry to die before I knew that he was saved. December 13, 2012, that happened. I must have asked God a thousand times, "Why?" My faith was shaken to its core. First of all, *I* was supposed to die first. My entire married life I thought that I would because I didn't want to live one second without him. Never in my wildest dreams did I ever entertain the thought of him leaving before me.

My daughter, Buddy, was in New York when her precious dad passed away. She flew down as fast as she could. I can't imagine how difficult that trip was for her nursing a broken heart.

Three days later, we had Larry's funeral. His obituary did not make our local paper in time, but it did in the FW Star-Telegram. As long as I live, I will never forget the 300 plus people who attended Larry's service. I remember that Sunday morning reading Jesus Calling for Dec. 16th and this Scripture: Isaiah 50:4 "The Lord has given me His words of wisdom so that I may know what I should say to all these weary ones. Morning by morning He awakens me and opens my understanding to His will." The kids and I decided to have a receiving line after Larry's service because we knew that many of those people who attended had driven hundreds of miles to pay their last respects.

I had asked my dear neighbor, Lee, a retired preacher, if he would give Larry's eulogy. He said yes, he would, and I can still hear him saying, "Thank you for asking me." I think that most people would have been so nervous to do so, but Lee was not. The day before his dad's service, Nick wrote a paper about his dad, walked across the street to Lee's house, and asked him if he would read this at the funeral. I had no idea that Nick had done this; I doubt there were very many dry eyes when Lee read:

Being alone for the first time in my life was a difficult transition for me to make. Now I had to take care of the house, yard, finances, everything, by myself. Many nights I would hear noises and be scared; my hero, my protector wasn't sleeping beside me anymore. Then God gave me this verse: Psalms 4:8 "I will lie down in peace and sleep, for though I am alone, O, Lord, you will keep me safe." I think that King David penned this verse when his enemies were near, and it brought him the same comfort that it brought me, and still does, all these years later.

For days, I was in a deep depression, not understanding why God would do this to me. Then one day, Karen, a precious Sunday school sister, came by to see me. When I cried and told her of my feelings, she said to me these life-changing words: "Our God is a loving God. He would **never** snatch Larry from you and throw him into hell." Her words brought so much comfort to me; they were just what I needed to bring me out of this dark hole I had descended into.

After Karen's visit, I thought about the two thieves on crosses beside Jesus as He was dying for our sins to be forgiven. One thief mocked Jesus; the other said, "Remember me when you get to your Kingdom." That was all it took to let Jesus know that this thief believed in Him. Jesus replied, "Today you will be with me in Paradise." I truly believe that before Larry lost consciousness, he called out to the Lord. Acts 2:21/ KJV says: "Whosoever shall call upon the name of the Lord shall be saved."

Even though I was say 95% sure that my Larry was in Heaven, there was that 5% weighing me down. So, one night as I was crying, I asked God to please give me a sign and to make it plain so that I would know beyond a shadow of a doubt that Larry was indeed in Heaven. The next morning, I remembered a religious email from a sweet friend with sayings and pictures that I had received the day before. One picture flashed before me, and I ran to the computer. I usually delete messages as soon as I read them, and much to my chagrin I had already done so concerning this one. I decided to try the Delete file, and it was still there!!! I clicked on it and scrolled through that message from the day before, and sure enough, there was that image I had remembered seeing. It made me cry, for sure, as my sign couldn't have been any plainer. This was the only sign I received from my Heavenly Father. I read this Bible verse soon afterwards: Matthew 6:8 "Your Father knows exactly what you need even before you ask Him!" God is SO good to me. I can rest assured that I will see Larry again someday in Heaven. Maybe we will even get to share a residence there with each other. Whatever God has planned will be wonderful; I am so blessed.

I never knew the profound grief one experiences when one loses a cherished spouse; now, I do. Death is so final, here on earth. I missed Larry's presence so much: his beautiful smile, wonderful sense of humor, his hugs, love, laughter, and care. He was the best husband, dad, grampa, and friend. He made me laugh virtually every day. I remember coming home from school my last year of teaching.

Larry had retired the year before. When I walked into the kitchen, he was standing there next to the stove. We stood chatting for a few minutes. I kept noticing him glancing at a covered pot on the stove. All of a sudden, I realized that he wanted me to notice the pot, too. I said, "Daddy! Did you cook dinner for us?" Unreal, as he never did unless he was outside grilling. I lifted up the lid, **and there was a banana, peel and all, inside!!!**" Larry was laughing so hard he was bent over! Now it was my turn to say, "Crack yourself up, why don't you? " ☺ Oh, how I miss my man...

Christmases are not the same without him. The first one was only 13 days after we lost him. My mind draws a blank on that one. . . Larry always made Christmases special for our family.

One year, we all decided to have a "White Elephant" Christmas so that we could cut down on the cost of this holiday. At first, we agreed to each contribute three gifts, none to exceed the $15 limit (any or all could be free, too!). After that first "White Elephant" Christmas, which was lots of fun, Buddy thought it might be even more fun if we had 3 categories for these gifts: make, buy, find (we added a 4th one later: funny). This must have happened the year Larry retired in 2005 because he asked me if I could bring my cassette recorder (do they even make those anymore?) home for him to borrow for a day. I had no clue that he was using this for his "make" category the upcoming Christmas. Nick chose a gift bag during the "White Elephant" gift exchange, and he got his dad's "make" gift: a cassette tape called, "Larry Sings Christmas/2005." What a HOOT! We put it on, and on one song he's serious singing (all a cappella, mind you) "O, Come, All Ye Faithful," and the next he's really getting into, "Grandma Got Run Over by a Reindeer!" And so it went. We were laughing **so hard**! Nick and his dad both fell over onto the floor, they were laughing so much. Larry was crying with hysterics! I can still see his face...pure joy and fun with his family that he loved so much.

I cried for Larry every day for 17 months. When I did, I would ask God to please wash His peace over me, and in a few minutes, I was better.

Psalms 34:18 says, "The Lord is close to those whose hearts are breaking." One day, I asked God to please take my tears away, and He did that, too. Oh, not all of them; I still break down and get ambushed sometimes, but I feel God's presence every day, holding my hand as we journey together to Heaven. John 16:22 – "You have sorrow now, but I will see you again, and then you will rejoice, and no one can rob you of that joy."

Before I come to the most important part of this book, I need to address two things that I mentioned earlier in this chapter. God promises not to give us more than we can bear. Even though I was so grief-stricken, my Heavenly Father was always close to me, helping me bear my sorrow. Luke 1:37: "For every promise from God shall surely come true." What would I have done without Him?

I also said that my faith was shaken to its core when I realized that Larry was gone, and I did not know where he was: Heaven or Hell. I never lost my faith, but it was strongly tested. Luke 7:23 came to me. Jesus said: "Blessed is the one who does not lose his faith in Me." Thank you, Jesus, for your constant presence in my life.

For several months, I had felt the Holy Spirit urging me to write this book. I fought doing so for quite a while, I am ashamed to say. Then I read this verse I had written on an index card soon after losing Larry: 1 Peter 2:9: "You have been chosen by God Himself so that you may show to others how God called you out of the darkness into His wonderful light." I never knew what a daunting task it is to write a book! Striving to put everything into chronological order in an autobiography is not easy, especially if the writer is a senior citizen. Our memories are dim, to say the least, but I had a lot of Divine inspiration helping me to get this book finished.

I truly believe that the main reason why I was called to write Journey to Heaven was to include the plan of salvation. We never know if we will be here from one *second* to the next. December 13, 2012, taught me that in a very personal way. We have a choice as to where we will spend eternity, either in Heaven or Hell. I used to think that Hell was this big lake with burning oil on its surface. I envisioned people standing around in it weeping and wailing, and gnashing their teeth like the Bible describes Hell. I was talking to someone about Hell one time, and this man said that he thought Hell would be solitary confinement for each occupant (no misery likes company existing there!) for ETERNITY! Forever and ever!

Then there's my vision of Heaven. Actually, I can't even begin to visualize the sheer beauty of it all, seeing Jesus first and getting the best hug EVER! Like the beautiful picture God gave me for my sign, the Pearly Gates will be behind Him, and I strongly believe I will see Larry there waiting for me to enter. We all have our own unique picture of Heaven. I think an angel with a big, booming voice announces each new arrival: "Larry Anderson is approaching the Pearrrrllllly Gates!!!" Everyone who is there who knew and loved Larry ran to the gates to hug him, love on him, and show him around his new Home. Everybody is nice in Heaven, so there won't be any fighting as to who our celestial escorts will be. ☺

Please don't delay another second if you are not saved or not sure. You can be sure and know beyond a shadow of a doubt that you will spend your eternity in Heaven with Jesus. Oh, the joys to come!

How to be saved and know for certain that you are going to spend eternity in Heaven:
Pray this prayer to Jesus, and He will come into your life right now:

Lord Jesus, I am a sinner and need to be saved. I admit that I cannot save myself. I accept your death and resurrection as payment for my sin. I repent of my sin. I open the door of my heart and invite you to come in. Thank you, Jesus, for hearing my prayer, saving me, and giving me eternal life. In your Name I pray, Amen.

If this prayer truly expresses the desire of your heart, you are saved. Right now! So, what does God expect of you now?

1. **Tell others about your decision.**
2. **Find a church to attend where the plan of Salvation is preached.**
3. **Show your faith in Christ by being baptized.**
4. **Pray, read your Bible, and share Jesus with others who need Him.**

When we go on a journey, we need a road map to show us the way. The Bible is our map along our journey to Heaven. Psalms 119:105/KJV says: "Thy Word is a lamp unto my feet and a light unto my path." I love to read my Bible; I learn something new every day. Find some quiet time to spend with Jesus. It will become the most important and best time of your day.

My little family and I have been through 8 December 13ths now. Father's Days are also tough on the kids and me. I told my friend, Marsh, on the first anniversary of Larry's death, how sad we were. She said something very profound to me. Marsh told me that she will not think of December 13th as the anniversaries of Larry's passing, but rather the anniversaries of his *ascension into Heaven*. Wow! I so needed that. The love and support of my dear family and friends during this sad part of my journey continues to bless me today.

Jesus is with you every day. Nothing will happen to you that you and He cannot handle...together! ☺ His Father, our Father, truly does not give us more than we can bear.

I want your journey to take you to Heaven. Don't look for my mansion. Look for the 2-story doghouse. I hope to see you there.

Psalm 40:1-3 - "I waited patiently for God to help me; then He listened and heard my cry. He lifted me out of the pit of despair, out from the bog and the mire, and set my feet on a hard, firm path, and steadied me as I walked along. He has given me a new song to sing, of praises to our God. Now many will hear of the glorious things He did for me, and stand in awe before the Lord, and put their trust in Him."

ABOUT THE AUTHOR

Rachel (a.k.a."Fluffy") grew up in Massachusetts with her Ma and Dad and 5 siblings. She married Larry (a.k.a. "Skeeter") and moved to a foreign country called Oklahoma and then on to the great state of Texas. She is a blessed mother, grandmother, sister, friend, gardener, hand quilter, retired elementary school teacher, squirrel catcher, and laughter advocate. Fluffy loves the Lord, reading her Bible, and thanking God for her many blessings every day.

CPSIA information can be obtained
at www.ICGtesting.com
Printed in the USA
BVHW030452200123
656704BV00003B/41